Measuring Up

Advances in How
We Assess Reading Ability

Edited by John P. Sabatini,
Elizabeth Albro, & Tenaha O'Reilly

ROWMAN & LITTLEFIELD EDUCATION

A division of
ROWMAN & LITTLEFIELD PUBLISHERS, INC.
Lanham • Boulder • New York • Toronto • Plymouth, UK

Published by Rowman & Littlefield Education
A division of Rowman & Littlefield Publishers, Inc.
A wholly owned subsidiary of The Rowman & Littlefield Publishing Group, Inc.
4501 Forbes Boulevard, Suite 200, Lanham, Maryland 20706
www.rowman.com

10 Thornbury Road, Plymouth PL6 7PP, United Kingdom

British Library Cataloguing in Publication Information Available

Library of Congress Cataloging-in-Publication Data

Measuring up : advances in how we assess reading ability / edited by John P. Sabatini,
Elizabeth Albro, and Tenaha O'Reilly.
       p. cm.
    Summary: "Measuring Up: Advances in How We Assess Reading Ability" addresses
the fundamental issues of measuring reading comprehension, in theory and in practice.
In light of federal legislation towards common core standards and assessments, as well
as significant national investments in reading and literacy education, it is a critical and
opportune time to bring together the research and measurement community to address
these issues" —Provided by publisher.
    ISBN 978-1-60709-485-2 (hardback) — ISBN 978-1-60709-486-9 (paper) — ISBN
978-1-60709-487-6 (electronic)
    1. Reading—Ability testing—United States. I. Sabatini, John P. II. Albro, Elizabeth,
1966- III. O'Reilly, Tenaha.
    LB1050.46.M43 2012
    372.48
                                                                2012010919

Printed in the United States of America

Literacy represents both a national aspiration and a set of human practices anchored in space and time. From this dual existence literacy has acquired both a sociopolitical dimension, associated with its role within society and the ways in which it is deployed for political, cultural, and economic ends; and a psychological dimension, associated with cognitive and affective properties that lead to greater or lesser individual motivation for and competence with writing and print.

—Richard L. Venezky, 1984

Contents

List of Figures   vii

List of Tables   ix

Preface   xi

Acknowledgments   xiii

Introduction   xv

SECTION I: DEVELOPING COHERENCE IN THE CONSTRUCT OF READING COMPREHENSION

1 Reading Comprehension: A Conceptual Framework from Word Meaning to Text Meaning   3
Charles Perfetti and Suzanne M. Adlof

2 Psychological Models of Reading Comprehension and Their Implications for Assessment   21
Walter Kintsch

3 Individual and Developmental Differences in Reading Comprehension: Assessing Cognitive Processes and Outcomes   39
Paul van den Broek

4 Reading Comprehension Development from Seven to Fourteen Years: Implications for Assessment   59
Kate Cain and Jane Oakhill

5   Measure for Measure: Challenges in Assessing Reading
       Comprehension   77
       Janice M. Keenan

6   Sources of Text Difficulty: Across Genres and Grades   89
       Danielle S. McNamara, Arthur Graesser, and Max Louwerse

**SECTION II: THE SCIENCE OF ASSESSMENT AND THE
                PROFICIENT READER**

7   How Research on Reading and Research on Assessment Are
       Transforming Reading Assessment (or if They Aren't, How
       They Ought To)   119
       Robert J. Mislevy and John P. Sabatini

8   Psychological versus Psychometric Dimensionality in Reading
       Assessment   135
       André A. Rupp

Conclusion: Moving Forward on Reading Assessment   153
       Arthur Graesser and Xiangen Hu

Measuring Up: Advances in How We Assess Reading Ability:
Editor Biographies   159

List of Figures

Figure 1.1.   Schematized model of comprehension components   4
Figure 2.1.   Situation models for a text on the circulatory system
               can be evaluated by drawing a diagram pre- and
               post-reading   31
Figure 4.1.   Path diagram illustrating the relations between skills
               from Time One to Time Three reading
               comprehension   69
Figure 6.1.   Local and global indices of referential and semantic
               cohesion as a function of genre and DRP grade level   100
Figure 6.2.   Verb cohesion as a function of genre and DRP grade
               level   104
Figure 6.3   Incidence of connectives as a function of genre and
               DRP grade level   105
Figure 6.4.   Causal cohesion as a function of genre and DRP
               grade level   106
Figure 7.1.   Structure for assessment arguments   122
Figure 8.1.   A visual representation of a cognitive framework for
               basic reading   137
Figure 8.2.   A visual representation of a cognitive framework for
               advanced reading / reading comprehension   139

List of Tables

Table 2.1.	The interaction between reading skills and domain knowledge	24
Table 2.2.	Inference types	27
Table 3.1.	Creating coherence during reading: Mechanisms and sources of activation	41
Table 4.1.	Typical characteristics of good and poor comprehenders matched for word reading and reading vocabulary knowledge, and a younger comprehension-age match group	61
Table 5.1.	Format features of our reading comprehension tests	80
Table 6.1.	Ranges of the DRP scores as a function of grade level categories	95
Table 6.2.	Descriptive statistics as a function of genre and DRP grade level	97
Table 6.3.	F table for cohesion indices	99
Table 6.4.	Cohesion indices as a function of DRP grade levels	101
Table 6.5.	Cohesion indices as a function of genre	102
Table 6.6.	Summary of results in terms of the five sources of text difficulty found for each of the three text genres	111
Table 8.1.	Summary of key design characteristics of studies with compensatory multidimensional IRT models	146
Table 8.2.	Summary of key design characteristics of studies with DCMs	147

Preface

Why should educators, administrators, and policy makers read books about reading assessment?

Stimulating educators' enthusiasm and interest in learning about assessments is as daunting a challenge as engaging the interest of adolescents in subject area content learning, but this subject is no less important to future success. The broader educational community needs to grapple with learning about the concepts in reading assessment books to gain a deeper understanding of what reading literacy is, how it develops, and what emerging measures and systems are being conceived as tools for engineering a more literate citizenry. The adaptation and adoption of these technologies into our social culture are no less important than the theory and technical expertise put into their design. The sharpened knife is a dangerous tool in untrained hands, just as much as the dull blade to the professional.

The contributors to these volumes have made an effort to use as little technical jargon as is necessary to explain complex concepts; they themselves come from different subdisciplines, so the need to create a common language is ever-present. We ask that the educated audience interested in reading literacy also take on the challenge of being thoughtful readers, accepting that in some cases technical knowledge and explanation is necessary to learning. We advise the reader to follow the chain of references to other sources to gain background knowledge when he or she perceives its absence. We feel that the content here is highly accessible and important, although not always simple to understand. We hope that with this volume, you join in the venture and that through your increased knowledge, increased participation in the process.

By working with the research and measurement specialists in whatever educational setting you inhabit, together we can craft effective, efficient tools and technologies that have more positive than negative impacts in the reading literacy skills of learners. We are all in this together.

Acknowledgments

This volume was preceded by a conference on Assessing Reading in the 21st Century, held in Philadelphia in April 2008. We are extremely grateful to the Institute of Education Sciences and Educational Testing Service for sponsoring and supporting this conference. We would also like to thank the many individuals who organized, presented, and served as discussants and as a rapt audience at the conference. We are grateful to the chapter reviewers for their dedication to the field, and to those who provided invaluable feedback along the way, and to Jennifer Lentini, for her work in coordinating, reviewing, and editing this volume. Finally, we would like to thank the authors who contributed chapters to this volume. Without the innovative work they have conducted in the areas of reading comprehension, reading assessment, and technology, this volume would not have been possible.

Introduction

Reading is both a simple and complex construct/concept. Like other complex concepts (e.g., "freedom"), people believe they know what it is, but most individuals probably would not agree on the meaning or understanding, and even more challenging (for measurement specialists), our definition of reading evolves and transforms itself across historical and developmental time. What we measure or strive for in reading proficiency for all students has changed from 1911 to 2011 and changes from first grade through postsecondary education.

What most educational researchers believe and most national surveys support, is the claim that far too many U.S. citizens read below their potential and below the proficiency levels our society aspires to make the standard. For example, an estimated 34 percent of fourth graders and 26 percent of eighth graders are in the Below Basic category on NAEP (National Center for Education Statistics, 2009). Among adults, approximately 12 percent of respondents scored Below Basic on the prose and document sections on the National Assessment of Adult Literacy (Kutner, Greenberg, & Baer, 2005).

Despite these statistics, the science of reading acquisition, processes, and individual differences in general and special populations has been continuously advancing through interdisciplinary research. These areas span cognitive, psycholinguistic (including computational linguistics), developmental, genetic, neuroscience, cross-language studies, and experimental comparison studies of effective instruction. Some of the science of reading has emerged from the theory and research into the realm of practice and policy as component processes of reading, such as phonemic awareness, decoding, fluency, vocabulary, and comprehension strategies. This transition from basic to applied knowledge has taken place, in large part, on the strength of the alignment of theoretical constructs to new *research* measures of those constructs.

In spite of these advances, the practice of measuring "reading comprehension" has remained relatively immune to much of this foundational knowledge. Most reading tests continue to rely on performance on a single series of questions asked about a series of passages, with the primary modern innovation seemingly to be the addition of constructed/written responses and rubric scores. Even as technologies and their cultural concomitants continue to change the shape of the literacy (and language) landscape at a pace unparalleled in human history—expanding some literacy practices (e.g., e-mail, instant messaging) and contracting others (e.g., handwritten letters)—our testing systems and instruments appear to be only modestly influenced by them.

Meanwhile, critical questions remain masked by these traditional assessment practices. Is, as one might believe based on the single scale score one receives on a state outcome exam, reading comprehension a unitary construct? Is it the same construct when viewed either vertically (developmentally) or laterally (across the various types of reading acts and texts individuals engage in to construct meaning for different goals)? What kinds of evidence and methods would help us answer such questions? What kinds of assessment tools will help advance educational policy and practice toward attaining higher reading comprehension achievement levels for all individuals?

In light of the significant national investments in reading and literacy education, it is a critical and opportune time to bring together leaders in the field to focus on reading assessment questions. The two volumes are divided into four sections. The first section of Volume 1, *Measuring Up: Advaces in How We Assess Reading Ability*, addresses the question of what reading comprehension is and how it develops or changes across time. The second section of Volume 1 introduces several innovations in ideas and technologies in the design and development of assessment as applied to the context of reading.

The first section of Volume 2, *Reaching an Understanding: Innovations in How We View Reading Assessment* includes all manner of applications of new assessment techniques in applied settings. Finally, in the second section of Volume 2, we present several chapters that discuss advanced psychometric techniques that are under development and have potentially transformative implications for how we design and interpret reading assessments. Together, these chapters provide both a primer for literacy assessment in the twenty-first century.

OVERVIEW OF VOLUME 1: SECTIONS I AND II

Section I: Developing Coherence in the Construct of Reading Comprehension

The astute reader will find many overlapping concepts and themes in the opening six chapters. In assessment terms, there is much convergence, or shared variance, which could be considered evidence of a main factor or construct of sorts. Of course, the authors are all familiar with each other's writings and research, so a reciprocally causal relation might be inferred. Interestingly, when the authors reference assessment concepts, they mostly reference other cognitive and reading research studies, which is in contrast to the references the reader will find when similar concepts are raised in the assessment chapters authored by measurement researchers in Section II.

We have not attempted to have the authors reduce this overlap for efficiency's sake, because we believe that the slightly different representations of the same concepts and themes will reinforce those ideas for the reader, as well as reveal the subtle differences in emphasis and approach that remain. There is shared and unique variance to be mined here.

For example, while all authors credit the importance of building a memory representation or situation model and acknowledge the moderating influence of automated and strategic skill processes in relation to capacity limitations, Kintsch puts greater emphasis on distinctions between the more literal textbase vs. the more knowledge- and inference-driven situation model, and the importance of knowledge in that construction; Perfetti and Adlof focus more attention on the access and quality of the relationships built up around words in a semantic neighborhood during construction of that model; van den Broek puts emphasis on the network nature of the representation that evolves over processing cycles during reading, and the control exerted by the individual via setting and adjusting standards of coherence to the comprehension problem. Still, all of these ideas drift through each chapter and if we were to mine the full works of each author (rather than limiting them to about fifteen pages), we would find fuller treatments of all concepts.

Some critics argue that traditional multiple-choice assessments of reading comprehension measure and encourage a fragmented, piecemeal understanding of text. However, deep comprehension involves capturing and connecting the key relations among the central ideas in text. van den Broek argues that reading comprehension assessments should examine both the products (or outcomes) of reading as well as the processes that derive them. By capturing both elements, assessments are in a better position to measure the type of relational information that is associated with building deep models of understanding.

According to van den Broek's model, comprehension is a cyclical process that involves both automatic and strategic coherence-building processes. Comprehension is said to be built "moment by moment" though automatic process such as the spread of activation from the current sentence to both prior sentences and background knowledge. Comprehension is also constructed though a strategic coherence-building processes that searches prior text and recruits background knowledge in relation to one's standard of coherence.

This standard of coherence is said to vary among people and tasks, but it has a critical impact on type and depth of the representation created; higher standards should lead to better representations. Assessment of reading comprehension should consider standards of coherence when making judgments about student reading proficiency.

Developmental studies of reading have often focused on unpacking the component skills necessary for "breaking the code," or learning how to decode printed text. We have a deep understanding now of how those skills emerge developmentally, and have a large number of reliable and valid assessment tools that can be used to identify where young students are struggling with mastery of decoding. However, our understanding of what components contribute primarily to comprehension and how they emerge over development is less elaborated.

Cain and Oakhill have been at the forefront in elucidating component skills of reading comprehension, and have described how the unique features of reading comprehension in school-aged readers develop. Their chapter provides a summary of their work to date and provides suggestions about which comprehension specific features should be incorporated into future assessments.

Leveraging the identification of poor readers whose struggles are located in comprehension difficulties rather than word reading difficulties, and using novel assessment techniques, Cain and Oakhill have been able to isolate several subskills that are differentially associated with poor comprehension. Those factors include inference and integration, comprehension monitoring, and the knowledge and use of narrative structure. They then describe the findings from a longitudinal study in which they explored whether these factors predict growth in reading comprehension. The developmental findings they report provide a compelling argument for assessing these skills as children begin to learn to read, and for using the outcomes of these assessments to shape instruction.

What do current measures of reading comprehension measure? Do measures used with different aged readers function in the same way? These are two of the questions that Keenan explores in her chapter, which reports a study that emerged out of a finding that intercorrelations among multiple reading comprehension tests were surprisingly low. There has only been one prior comparison of reading comprehension tests used in the United States, and the differences found in that study were substantially smaller than those described here.

As is apparent across all of the chapters in this volume, researchers are deeply interested in understanding what skills contribute to reading comprehension and how those skills are to be measured. Keenan finds that assumptions made about readers' comprehension skills must also take into account features of the assessment tool, including formatting features such as passage length. Importantly, these formatting features are correlated with the target age of the reader, and with whether the comprehension measure is highly related to or independent of decoding skill. Keenan's findings suggest constraints on the types of conclusions about reading comprehension that can be drawn for tests designed for younger and less skilled readers.

Reading ability represents a complex interaction between reader characteristics, task expectations, and text complexity. While there has been a lot of research on reader characteristics, much less attention has been given to issues surrounding how linguistic features contribute to text complexity. Traditionally, text complexity has been dominated by unidimensional readability measures such as Flesch-Kincaid reading ease or grade level. These measures rely heavily on indices of word frequency and sentence length to derive a single measure of difficulty.

Recognizing the potential for greater precision, McNamara and her colleagues have designed an automated tool called Coh-Metrix that produces a broader array of text complexity indices. Coh-Metrix measures a large number of linguistic features such as connectives, local/global/verb cohesion, and casual ratio index to provide a fine grain of linguistic detail. Using these measures, McNamara, Graesser, and Louwerse were able to show that text features interact as a function of grade level and genre—a result that would not have been impossible if text complexity was measured with traditional, unidimensional indices. With more precise text indices at hand, researchers and practitioners can do a better job of maximizing learning experiences by assessing text by reader skill interactions.

Section II: The Science of Assessment and the Proficient Reader

The field of reading comprehension assessment has been primarily dominated by measurement models that maximize item discrimination on a single factor scale of reading. When items fail to load on this single factor, assessment developers search for cognitive explanations to explain why an item did not function properly. Before the 1990s, cognitive explanations of student reading performance were often treated as an afterthought in the design of reading assessments.

In contrast to this traditional approach, Mislevy and Sabatini propose an alternative solution that integrates cognitive theory within assessment design. Rather than ignore the rich literature on reading, the authors argue integrating this work into the design of the assessment *before* the test has been developed using an evidence-centered design (ECD) approach.

With a solid foundation in cognitive science, assessments have the potential of being more meaningful and informative for instructional purposes. In an elaboration of the ECD model, Mislevy and Sabatini propose the idea of treating assessment as a form of argument. This "assessment as argument" approach advocates the creation of both design and use case arguments. These arguments not only ground claims with data, but also contextualize them with reading theory, task features, and evaluation procedures. With these use cases in mind, researchers and practitioners are better informed about the purposes of the assessment, including its intended uses, potential misuses, and instructional implications.

Most measurement models applied to reading comprehension assessments are unidimensional in nature, while most cognitive theories of reading often imply a multidimensional framework. This paradox in capability and practice is problematic for moving the field of reading assessment forward. To reconcile these issues, many researchers have begun to develop diagnostic classification models to account for the multidimensional nature of reading theory.

While there has been a lot of enthusiasm surrounding the promise of these models, Rupp argues that the enthusiasm should be contextualized by the available evidence. Rupp reviews the existing evidence gathered though both simulation and human data studies and concludes that more research is needed before we can conclusively use these models with a high degree of confidence. Although most of the research on multidimensional IRT exists in domains other than reading (e.g., math), the available evidence points to only two or three separable dimensions. Even so, these separable dimensions remain highly correlated.

While some may view these results as discouraging, the results in no way detract from the value of improving reading assessment by integrating cognitive theory into the assessment design. Dimensions are certainly useful for reporting purposes, but the benefits of integrating cognitive theory go beyond reporting. For instance, incorporating empirically-validated reading strategies into the design, as advocated by Sheehan and O'Reilly in *Reaching an Understanding*, may impact consequential validity. When reading strategies appear in the assessment, it may perhaps encourage their use in the classroom. These intended consequences could have beneficial impacts on instruction.

REFERENCES

Kutner, M., Greenberg, E., & Baer, J. (2005). *A first look at the literacy of America's adults in the 21st century* (NCES 2006-470). Washington DC: National Center for Education Statistics, Institute of Educations Sciences, U.S. Department of Education.

National Center for Education Statistics (2009). *The Nation's Report Card: Reading 2009* (NCES 2010–458). Washington, DC: Institute of Education Sciences, U.S. Department of Education.

Section I

DEVELOPING COHERENCE IN THE CONSTRUCT OF READING COMPREHENSION

Chapter One

Reading Comprehension: A Conceptual Framework from Word Meaning to Text Meaning

Charles Perfetti & Suzanne M. Adlof[1]

Reading comprehension is widely agreed to be not one, but many things. At the least, it is agreed to entail cognitive processes that operate on many different kinds of knowledge to achieve many different kinds of reading tasks. Emerging from the apparent complexity, however, is a central idea: Comprehension occurs as the reader builds one or more mental representations of a text message (e.g., Kintsch & Rawson, 2005). Among these representations, an accurate model of the situation described by the text (Van Dijk & Kintsch, 1983) is the product of successful deep comprehension.

A COMPONENTIAL FRAMEWORK FOR COMPREHENSION

The comprehension processes that bring about these mental representations occur at multiple levels across units of language: word-level (lexical processes), sentence-level (syntactic processes), and text-level. Across these levels, processes of word identification, parsing, referential mapping, and inference all contribute, interacting with the reader's conceptual knowledge to produce a situation model of the text. Figure 1.1 represents the components of comprehension in a way that is probably more orderly than how they exist in reality. Even so, the framework is useful for providing a freeze-frame view, necessary to address issues of assessments in any way short of tools that could capture the dynamics of real-time processing.

Figure 1.1 includes two major classes of processes along with linguistic and conceptual knowledge sources. The processes involve: (1) the identification of words and (2) the engagement of language-processing mechanisms that assemble these words into messages. These processes provide contextually appropriate word meanings, parse word strings into constituents, and provide

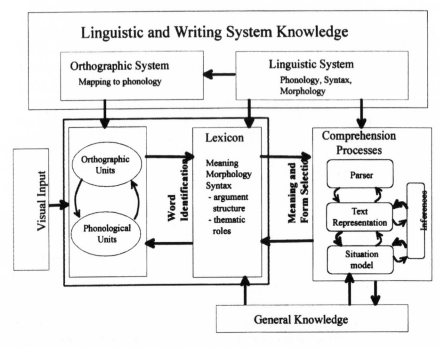

Figure 1.1.   Schematized model of comprehension components.

inferential integration of sentence information into more complete representations of extended text. These representations are critically enhanced by other knowledge sources.

SKILL IN COMPREHENSION COMPONENTS

In this framework, all the processes and component knowledge sources become points of interest for analysis and assessment of comprehension skill. In fact, the knowledge sources can be so general that comprehension can resemble general intelligence, entailing highly general processing constraints (e.g., working memory, retrieval speed) along with the use of general conceptual knowledge. But conflating comprehension with cognition carries costs to conceptual clarity. One cost is the loss of a focus for assessment. Indeed, variability of focus is the current state of affairs among published reading comprehension assessments, each of which differ in the degree to which they test word reading, background knowledge, and inference skills (Bowyer-Crane & Snowling, 2005; Coleman, Lindstrom, Nelson, Lindstrom, & Gregg, 2010;

Cutting & Scarborough, 2006; Francis, Fletcher, Catts & Tomblin, 2005; Keenan, Betjemann & Olson, 2008).

Such variability may be inevitable, given different beliefs about what comprehension is and what parts of it can be efficiently measured. However, adopting a conceptual framework for comprehension components that reflects both theory and evidence is valuable in guiding assessment. Use of the framework can make clear which components are being assessed and which are not. An assessment that makes its focal points clear is useful to test consumers (e.g., teachers, parents, and administrators) and researchers.

It is unlikely that all components are equally important for variability in overall skill, equally independent, and equally measurable with conventional assessments. Each of these three considerations (skill-related variability, independence, and measurability) constitutes a reasonable criterion for nominating a component for assessment.

In this context, the first criterion, skill-related variability, is important in identifying "pressure points" in the comprehension system. A pressure point must have face validity as an intrinsic component of comprehension, as opposed to being only a correlate. It should also pass an additional test: showing robust variation among individuals that is associated with overall comprehension skill. Lastly, test consumers are often interested in tests that can identify targets for instruction and intervention; thus, all other things being equal, components that represent malleable targets for intervention would have priority over other components that might not be malleable targets.

In the following discussion, we briefly review some of the components that have attracted research on individual differences and thus may be pressure points that make a difference in overall comprehension skill. If so, they meet one of the main criteria for inclusion in comprehension assessments.

Word Identification

We begin with the lower-level components in the left-center part of the framework diagram in Figure 1.1. Word identification is a critical first component of reading comprehension. Substantial correlations between word reading ability and comprehension are observable widely across age ranges, even into adulthood (Adlof, Catts, & Little, 2006; Bell & Perfetti, 1994; Braze, Tabor, Shankweiler, & Mencl, 2007; Perfetti, 1985; Sabatini, 2002; Sabatini, 2003). But while any single component, including word identification skill, may be necessary, it may not be sufficient by itself for comprehension. Some components may not even be necessary for shallow levels of comprehension.

Until recently, the bulk of research investigating sources of reading difficulties focused solely on word reading. However, in recent years, it has become clear that some children and adults display *specific* problems with reading comprehension. That is, they show low reading comprehension performance in spite of seemingly adequate word reading skills (Catts, Adlof, & Ellis Weismer, 2006; Hart, 2005; Landi, 2010; Nation & Snowling, 1999; Yuill & Oakhill, 1991). The existence of this subgroup of individuals suggests that additional sources of comprehension problems are implicated. Our goal in the remainder of this chapter is to explore some of these additional sources of difficulty.

It is important, however, that examinations of these additional sources of difficulty take word identification into account. Higher-level components of comprehension depend on the effective operation of lower-level components, including word reading. The research on comprehension skill has been inconsistent in the extent to which it takes these dependencies into account.

As we review studies in the next section, we use two different labels to refer to individuals with reading comprehension difficulties. We use "SCD" (specific comprehension difficulties) to refer to participants in studies whose selection criteria required low skill in reading comprehension relative to word reading skills. [2] We use "less skilled comprehenders" to refer to participants in studies where word reading ability may have varied or was not explicitly controlled.

HIGHER-LEVEL COMPONENTS OF COMPREHENSION

Most of the research on individual differences in reading comprehension has focused on higher-level components, such as those comprehension processes in the right-center of Figure 1.1. These higher-level processes are at work as the reader recognizes words, retrieves their context-appropriate meanings, and builds phrases (parsing) from words. Thus, they depend on the operation of the lower-level components of Figure 1.1. Accordingly, making strong inferences about skill problems in higher-level processes requires the assumption that the lower-level processes are operating smoothly.

Although much of the research targeting higher-level processes as the source of comprehension problems has not met this assumption, some studies have tried to meet it, providing leads on higher-level pressure points in comprehension. For example, studies by Oakhill, Cain and colleagues have implicated higher-level comprehension problems by matching readers with SCD with control groups of skilled comprehenders on both word reading accuracy and print vocabulary knowledge (e.g., Cain & Oakhill, 1999; Cain, Oakhill, Barnes, & Bryant, 2001; Cataldo & Oakhill, 2000; Oakhill, 1984; Oakhill, Hart, & Samols, 2005).

With either sample—readers with SCD or less skilled comprehenders—research has been directed at a number of higher-level comprehension components. We next review three of those: inference making, comprehension monitoring, and comprehension strategy usage.

Inferences

To make sense of a text, skilled readers make inferences that bridge elements in the text or otherwise support the coherence necessary for comprehension. Inferences come in a variety of forms, with various taxonomies proposed (e.g., Graesser, Singer, & Trabasso, 1994; Zwaan & Radvansky, 1998). Most important for routine comprehension are inferences that help the reader build a coherent mental representation of the text.

For example, skilled readers form causal inferences to help make sense of actions in a story, even when those actions are not explicitly connected syntactically (Graesser & Kreuz, 1993; Trabasso & Suh, 1993). However, skilled readers do not make predictive and other elaborative inferences routinely because such inferences are not compelled by a need for either textual or causal coherence (Graesser et al., 1994; McKoon & Ratcliff, 1992). In sum, readers are more likely to make inferences that support coherence than those that merely elaborate.

Several studies have shown that children with SCD have more difficulty making inferences than do skilled comprehenders (e.g., Cain & Oakhill, 1999; Oakhill, 1984; Cain et al., 2001). Because inferences are triggered by missing or inexplicit elements of the text, one important aspect of inference making is the availability and accessibility of the background knowledge required to draw the inference.

Such background knowledge is another example of a component that is necessary but not sufficient for comprehension. For example, by teaching children knowledge about a novel situation, Cain & Oakhill (1999) and Cain et al. (2001) attempted to control for potential differences in background knowledge. They concluded that even when knowledge availability was controlled, children with SCD still displayed difficulty in making inferences. What else children with SCD need to support their reading remains an open question, but one likely candidate is help in setting high enough standards for coherence (van den Broek, 2012; van den Broek, Risden, & Husebye-Hartman, 1995).

Comprehension Monitoring

Comprehension monitoring allows the reader to verify his or her understanding and to make repairs where this understanding fails. The research has produced ample examples of failures by skilled adults (Glenberg, Wilkinson, & Epstein, 1982), as well as children (Baker, 1984; Garner, 1980) to monitor comprehension, with differences found across age and skill levels (Hacker, 1997).

Monitoring comprehension is not a single skill that is simply added to basic comprehension processes; rather, it depends in part on the reader's ability to construct an accurate representation of the sentences in the text (Otero & Kintsch, 1992; Vosniadou, Pearson, & Rogers, 1988). As is true for inferences, retrieval of knowledge (from memory of the text or from general background knowledge) is necessary for monitoring whether a text makes sense.

Although most research on comprehension monitoring has not controlled for lower-level skills, a few recent studies have employed behavioral and eye-tracking methods to examine comprehension monitoring children with SCD (Oakhill et al., 2005; van der Schoot, Vasbinder, Horsely, Reijntjes & van Lieshout, 2009). These studies find that children with SCD are less effective than skilled comprehenders at monitoring their own comprehension. Thus, at least some children with SCD not only gain less knowledge from text, they are also less aware of inconsistencies in the text and of instances where they fail to understand.

As is the case with inference making, the reader's standard for text coherence is relevant. It is only by expecting a text to make sense that a reader can notice when it does not. A reader's standard for coherence can change as a function of circumstances that affect his or her interest or engagement with a text.

This may imply that some differences in monitoring are situational rather than stable individual trait effects. A trait hypothesis would seem to assume that some readers have a dysfunction in a "monitoring system." A more likely alternative in our opinion is that to the extent poor monitoring is an individual trait, it reflects that less skilled comprehenders have become accustomed to not understanding texts, meaning they have adopted a low standard for coherence.

Comprehension Strategies

Skilled readers implicitly use strategies in comprehension. These strategies can be considered adjustments to reading procedures that reflect the reader's goals, the difficulty of the text, or some combination of the two. For example, readers can slow down to increase their understanding of a text or speed up (i.e., skim the text) to search for information. A broader view is seen in the research on teaching comprehension strategies, in which strategies are viewed not only as implicit adjustments to goals and texts, but also as explicit procedures to enhance comprehension. The National Reading Panel (2000) identified seven strategies for which there was sufficient evidence that direct instruction supported comprehension gain: (1) comprehension monitoring; (2) cooperative learning; (3) use of graphic and semantic organizers (e.g., story maps); (4) question answering; (5) question generation; (6) story structure; and (7) summarization. With the exception of comprehension monitoring, we have not identified any of these strategies as pressure points for comprehension assessment. They do not correspond to components of comprehension per se but to comprehension outcomes (e.g., summarization, question generation) or supports (e.g., organizers, cooperative learning). The use of these kinds of explicit strategies may be helpful to the reader in enhancing comprehension (e.g., Kletzien, 1991; Olshavsky, 1977; Wilson & Rupley, 1997), but they are not intrinsic to it.

WORD MEANINGS AND TEXT INTEGRATION

In the research on higher-level comprehension, only a few studies have controlled for knowledge of word meanings. Our view is that word meanings provide an especially potent pressure point among the components of comprehension; in the remainder of this chapter, we turn our attention to this component (shown in the center section of Figure 1.1).

Vocabulary

There are numerous studies that demonstrate a strong relationship between vocabulary knowledge and reading comprehension in both children and adults (e.g., Anderson & Freebody, 1981; Braze et al., 2007; Muter, Hulme, Snowling, & Stevenson, 2004; Storch & Whitehurst, 2002; Wagner, 2005). According to an estimate by Nagy and Scott (2000), a reader needs to know the meanings of 90 percent of the individual words contained within a text in order to comprehend it.

Most studies of the association between vocabulary knowledge and comprehension have used assessments of vocabulary size, such as the *Peabody Picture Vocabulary Test* (PPVT) (Dunn & Dunn, 2007) or the *Expressive Vocabulary Test* (Williams, 2007). Although vocabulary size, or lexical *quantity*, is important, successful comprehension also involves having refined knowledge of words and their relationships to other words (e.g., Nagy & Herman, 1987).

The lexical quality hypothesis claims that successful comprehension depends on accessible, well specified, and flexible knowledge of word forms and meanings (Perfetti & Hart, 2001; Perfetti, 2007). Lexical quality varies across individuals (some people know more about a larger number of words than others), as well as between words in a given individual's lexicon.

For example, some people have a richer representation of the meaning for the word "health" than for the related but less familiar word "salubrious." They may recall that salubrious is associated in some way with health, but they may not know whether it is associated with promoting good health (yes) or poor health (no). They may be able to understand a sentence containing either word, but they may not feel comfortable using "salubrious" in their own sentence constructions.

A high-quality meaning representation includes complete knowledge of relevant semantic attributes as well as sufficient experience in context to support knowledge of appropriate usages and associations. However, the separation of quantity and quality of word knowledge is not straightforward. Indeed, we should expect the number of words known to some minimal standard (*lexical quantity*) and the degree of knowledge about a given word (*lexical quality*) to be closely related on both statistical and cognitive grounds. The more words one knows, the more interconnections there will be among words.

In the case of word meaning (as opposed to word form), this quantity/quality distinction is often operationalized as a distinction of *breadth* (quantity) vs. *depth* (quality) of vocabulary. Breadth vs. depth was the subject of two studies examining their relative contributions to reading comprehension in elementary school-aged children.

Ouellette (2006) examined this question in a sample of sixty fourth-grade students. After controlling for the effects of nonverbal IQ, decoding, and word reading ability, the study determined that only vocabulary depth accounted for unique variance in comprehension. Both breadth and depth explained unique variance when word and nonword reading were not included in the model, but the contribution of depth was much larger than breadth.

Tannenbaum, Torgesen, and Wagner (2006) examined this question in a sample of more than 200 third-graders and found that both breadth and depth accounted for unique variance; however, the unique contribution of breadth was larger, and the unique contribution of depth failed to reach statistical significance. The studies agreed that most of the variance was shared between breadth and depth.

Several differences between the studies might be relevant for understanding how contrasting answers to a question like this can emerge. For example, comprehension tests vary in which components of comprehension receive implicit focus, and the two studies used very different types of comprehension assessments. In the Ouellette et al. study, comprehension was assessed using the Passage Comprehension subtest of the *Woodcock Reading Mastery Test-*

Revised (Woodcock, 1998), a cloze task that has been shown to be especially dependent on word-level knowledge (Francis et al., 2005).

In contrast, Tannenbaum and colleagues measured comprehension using the *Florida Comprehensive Assessment Test* (Florida Department of Education, 2005) and the *Stanford Achievement Test-9* (Harcourt Assessment, 1996), which use longer text passages that involve greater dependence on higher-level comprehension components. Thus, in the Ouellette et al. study, understanding of the short passages was more likely to hinge on the knowledge of a specific word, whereas in the Tannenbaum study, understanding of the text required integration of ideas across the texts.

Although the two studies defined vocabulary breadth and depth similarly, their divergent results were also likely caused by differences in the way these constructs were measured. Across both studies, all but one of the tasks were taken from standardized assessments with adequate reliability. Ouellette and colleagues' breadth tasks assessed children's ability to match pictures with spoken words and to name pictures. Their depth task measured children's ability to generate definitions of words that included relevant semantic features. Tannenbaum et al.'s latent construct of breadth included two measures: one was a word-picture matching test similar to one of Ouellette et al.'s breadth tasks, but the other involved a definitions task similar to Ouellette and colleagues' *depth* task.

Tannenbaum et al.'s latent depth construct included four tasks, which required students to provide synonyms that represent multiple aspects of a word's meaning, list semantic features of words, use target words in sentences, and provide lists of category members, respectively. An examination of the correlation matrices in the Tannenbaum et al. study reveals that the correlation between the breadth measures is much higher (.75) than the intercorrelations among the depth measures (ranging from .28 to .38); furthermore, the correlations between the individual measures of breadth with individual measures of depth were higher (ranging from .39 to .61) than the correlations of the depth measures with themselves. Thus, Tannenbaum et al.'s findings demonstrate how difficult it is to measure vocabulary depth separately from breadth.

Although additional research may clarify the quantity-quality relationship, it is possible that the natural correlation between the two may reduce the practical value of separation as vocabulary measures. Quantity statistically predicts quality. Acquiring deep knowledge of a word naturally builds on an earlier familiarity of the word form and meaning.

However, whether quantity and quality can be psychometrically separated is only part of the story. During reading it is the reader's knowledge of the form and meaning of a specific word—lexical quality—that matters, not the estimated size of the reader's vocabulary. Thus lexical quality plays a distinctive role in comprehension. In the following section, we review studies in which skilled and less skilled comprehenders appear to differ in their processing of highly familiar words.

LEXICAL KNOWLEDGE

An elaboration of lexical quality includes a core of semantic, syntactic, and morphological attributes along with conditions that allow constrained flexibility of use (as metaphors, for example). In the context of comprehension skill, studies have been largely restricted to measures of meaning attributes, assessed through associative and conceptual structures defined over links to other words.

Two such studies have explored the nature of word knowledge problems for SCD samples by comparing categorical semantic relations with simple associative relations. Nation and Snowling (1999) found that ten-year-olds with SCD showed priming for words that were either functionally related (e.g., SHAMPOO—HAIR) or highly associated category members (e.g., BROTHER—SISTER), but not for category members with low association strength (e.g., COW—GOAT).

Landi and Perfetti (2007) also studied meaning judgments using event-related potentials (ERPs)[3] and found that SCD adults showed a smaller relatedness effect in ERP components (P200 and N400) compared with skilled comprehenders. In contrast to the result of Nation and Snowling (1999), Landi and Perfetti (2007) found ERP skill differences for associatively related as well as categorically related words.

Whatever the reason for the different results concerning associative relations—a greater sensitivity of ERPs to associative strength, differences in mode of presentation (auditory vs. visual), or participant ages—the larger point is that the two studies converge to suggest that SCD readers have lower-quality semantic representations (weaker connections to other words) than skilled readers, even for relatively frequent words that are within their functional lexicons.

WORD-TO-TEXT INTEGRATION

In addition to semantic processing at the word level, recent studies using ERPs have demonstrated on-line text comprehension differences between skilled and less skilled adult readers that implicate the processing of word meanings (Yang, Perfetti & Schmalhofer, 2005, 2007). ERP components (especially the N400, a sensitive indicator of integration difficulty) showed the key difference during the reading of a word that must be linked to a referent established in a previous sentence (thus, word-to-text integration).

For example, consider the text segment: *After being dropped from the plane, the bomb hit the ground and blew up. The <u>explosion</u>* . . . The reader needs to link the word *explosion* with an event established by the main clause of the first sentence (the bomb blew up). In effect, the reader must treat *explosion* as a paraphrase of *blew up.*

The N400s observed in these studies indicate this paraphrase mapping works fine—easy integration—for skilled comprehenders, but not for less skilled comprehenders. When the words were identical in their lexical stem (*exploded* in the first sentence and *explosion* in the second), comprehension skill differences were not found. Thus, the skill difference seems to involve understanding one word in relation to the referential meaning established by a different word—a paraphrase comprehension factor.

Successful paraphrase comprehension is not about synonyms. Paraphrases in these integration studies represent a wide range of semantic relations. For example, in another text, readers must link *emergency room* in sentence 1 and *hospital* in sentence 2, two phrases that show a part–whole semantic relationship. Emergency rooms are in hospitals, so the mention of an emergency room enables immediate use of the word *hospital.*

Other relations can be present as well, as illustrated by this example: *Brad fumbled through the dark until he located the box of matches and struck one. After <u>lighting</u> the match, it was easier to see.* If one strikes a match successfully, he or she has lit the match. Still, *strike* and *light* are not synonyms, but, rather, refer to the same event in this context.

In general, the meaning processes of "paraphrase" require the selection of word meanings that are appropriate for a given context. What this means exactly needs to be worked out. If word meaning representations include episodic histories with the word in its contexts, as proposed by Bolger, Balass, Landen and Perfetti (2008), then flexibility of meaning usage is partly based on contextual histories. Such a conceptualization is also consistent with thinking about meaning as situated in a massively multidimensional space of the sort generated through *Latent Semantic Analysis* (LSA) and related algorithms.

The relationship between word knowledge and comprehension skill needs more research, especially at the more fine-grain levels of word knowledge that are reflected in the studies we have reviewed here. Nevertheless, an important conclusion so far is that SCD and less skilled readers show less detailed, less flexible, and/or less connected representations even for words that they know. Thus the word-level knowledge relevant for comprehension includes lexical quality as well as quantity.

From a vocabulary assessment perspective, it remains to be determined whether assessments of fine-grain semantic knowledge do a better job of predicting reading comprehension difficulties than do assessments of vocabulary size. Quantity measures, as we noted above, may prove sufficient for most purposes, because they estimate the number of words that a reader knows, and words of high quality are a subset of that number. We emphasize again, however, that for any encounter with a given text, it is the quality of the reader's word knowledge (form as well as meaning) for the words in that text that is crucial to comprehension.

LINKS TO ASSESSMENT

The componential framework gives a general picture of comprehension from the word identification level through various higher-level processes that are needed for comprehension at the deeper levels (i.e., building a situation model) as well as more superficial levels (e.g., parsing a sentence). The framework provides a set of "pressure points" in text comprehension, components of comprehension that meet three criteria: (1) face validity as an intrinsic component of comprehension as opposed to a correlate of comprehension and (2) robust variation among individuals in the component that is (3) associated with overall comprehension skill.

Any pressure point that meets these criteria is a candidate for assessment. The components of word identification, lexical quantity and quality, inference making, and comprehension monitoring all meet these criteria. So do other components we have not discussed—for example, the ability to recall a brief segment of text, a clause or a sentence, more or less verbatim (the contents of a text working memory that is involved with the text representation in Figure 1.1); or the ability to recognize when two syntactic strings converge on a similar meaning relation (e.g., a longer form of paraphrase than we have previously described) as well as other tests of sentence-parsing processes.

However, as a practical matter, candidates for assessment may need to meet other criteria beyond independent and measurable skill-related variability. These other criteria will vary according to the test purpose. For example, if the purpose of assessment is to identify sources of comprehension difficulty, the assessment needs to meet all of the criteria above, but possibly not any others. However, if the goal of assessment is to identify targets for instruction or intervention, one would add the criterion that the assessed components are amenable to instruction.

Although it is likely that all components of comprehension are acquired largely (identifying printed words) or partly (parsing) through learning, decisions on priorities for instruction take into account additional factors. Some processes are distinct to reading, e.g., word identification. Other processes, e.g. working memory, are general to cognitive functioning. In between are processes that are largely shared between written and spoken language (e.g., parsing and inference making).

In deciding for intervention to increase working memory, one is making a bet on improving functioning broadly across cognitive tasks. Although this bet might pay off (Chein & Morrison, 2010), there is more certainty (and face validity) for instruction on components that are more directly about reading. However, assessments need not be only about diagnosing component weaknesses, whether general cognitive functions such as working memory or specific reading components such as word identification.

An important value of assessment can be to predict risk for reading comprehension difficulties. In this case a "good" assessment is simply one with high sensitivity and specificity (cf. Adlof, Catts, & Lee, 2010). Although determining priorities for assessment entails all these considerations, and probably more, it is important in the long run to have valid assessments for all the components identified in Figure 1.1. The fact that, at the moment, instructional prospects for the components vary is a different matter. Instructional interventions can be improved, and one of the engines for their improvement is valid assessments.

In terms of test efficiency, it may also be useful to ask whether the component is theoretically and empirically dependent on some other component. All components in an interactive system will show some degree of nonindependence. Figure 1.1 shows a number of two-way interactive connections that would multiply the interdependence between components. (With some constraints, these interactions would show more dependence of higher levels on lower levels than vice versa.) This interdependence seems to limit the goal of any pure, single-component assessment, instead supporting the assumption that all task performance depends on multiple components. Nevertheless, the degree of dependence among components is variable, both theoretically and as a question of assessment.

At higher levels of reading comprehension, lower levels are participating fully, whether they are assessed or not. A standard reading comprehension test may not measure word identification, but performance on the test requires it. At lower levels, word identification is best measured by presenting isolated words, thus assuring that both the process and the assessment is free of higher-level influences. (Note that word identification depends on visual and phonological abilities not assessed on the same test.)

The variability in interdependence allows for a component sampling strategy: Assess with a small sample of modestly related components rather than a large number of highly related components. This increases the efficiency, understood as an assessment's ability to measure distinctive components of comprehension in relation to testing time.

Of course, there are additional problems of assessment (e.g., models of item selection and other psychometric issues) that are beyond what we can address here. We believe that reading comprehension researchers can play a productive role in working with assessment experts on these problems, however. A framework for the components of comprehension with pressure points identified is a starting point. Alignment to assessment strategies is the next step.

REFERENCES

Adlof, S. M. (2010). Morphosyntactic skills in poor comprehenders. *Dissertation Abstracts International-B, 70*(8).

Adlof, S. M., Catts, H. W., & Lee, J. (2010). Kindergarten predictors of second vs. eighth grade reading comprehension impairments. *Journal of Learning Disabilities, 43*, 332–45.

Adlof, S. M., Catts, H. W., & Little, T. D. (2006). Should the simple view of reading include a fluency component? *Reading and Writing, 19*, 933–58.

Anderson, R. C., & Freebody, P. (1981) Vocabulary knowledge. In J. T. Guthrie (Ed.), *Comprehension and teaching: Research reviews* (pp. 77–117). Newark, DE: International Reading Association.

Baker, L. (1984). Spontaneous versus instructed use of multiple standards for evaluating comprehension: Effects of age, reading proficiency, and type of standard. *Journal of Experimental Child Psychology, 38*, 289–311.

Bell, L. C., & Perfetti, C. A. (1994). Reading skill: Some adult comparisons. *Journal of Educational Psychology, 86*, 244–55.

Bolger, D. J., Balass, M., Landen, E., & Perfetti, C. A. (2008). Context variation and definitions in learning the meanings of words: An instance-based learning approach. *Discourse Processes, 45*, 122–59.

Bowyer-Crane, C., & Snowling, M. J. (2005). Assessing children's inference generation: what do tests of reading comprehension measure? *British Journal of Educational Psychology, 75*, 189–201.

Braze, D., Tabor, W., Shankweiler, D. P., & Mencl, W. E. (2007). Speaking up for vocabulary: Reading skill differences in young adults. *Journal of Learning Disabilities, 40*, 226–43.

Cain, K., & Oakhill, J. V. (1999). Inference ability and its relation to comprehension failure in young children. *Reading and Writing, 11*, 489–503.

Cain, K., Oakhill, J. V., Barnes, M. A., & Bryant, P. E. (2001). Comprehension skill, inference-making ability, and the relation to knowledge. *Memory and Cognition, 29*, 850–59.

Cataldo, M.G. & Oakhill, J.V. (2000) Why are poor comprehenders inefficient searchers? An investigation into the effects of text representation and spatial memory on ability to locate information in a text. *Journal of Educational Psychology, 92,* 791–99.

Catts, H. W., Adlof, S. M., & Ellis Weismer, S. (2006). Language deficits in poor comprehenders: a case for the simple view of reading. *Journal of Speech Language and Hearing Research, 49,* 278–93.

Chein, J. M. & Morrison, A.B (2010). Expanding the mind's workspace: Training and transfer effects with a complex working memory span task. *Psychonomic Bulletin & Review 17,* 193–99.

Coleman, C., Lindstrom, J., Nelson, J., Lindstrom, W., & Gregg, K. N. (2010). Passageless comprehension on the *Nelson-Denny Reading Test:* Well above chance for university students. *Journal of Learning Disabilities, 43,* 244–49.

Cutting, L. E., & Scarborough, H. S. (2006). Prediction of reading comprehension: Relative contributions of word recognition, language proficiency, and other cognitive skills can depend on how comprehension is measured. *Scientific Studies of Reading, 10,* 277–99.

Dunn, L.M., & Dunn, D.M. (2007). *Peabody Picture Vocabulary Test-Fourth Edition.* Circle Pines, MN: American Guidance Service.

Florida Department of Education. (2005). *The new FCAT NRT: Stanford Achievement Test Series, Tenth Edition.* Tallahassee: State of Florida, Department of Education.

Francis, D., Fletcher, J. M., Catts, H. W., & Tomblin, J. B. (2005). Dimensions affecting the assessment of reading comprehension. In S. G. Paris & S. A. Stahl (Eds.), *Children's reading comprehension and assessment* (pp. 369–94). Mahwah, NJ: Lawrence Erlbaum Associates.

Garner, R. (1980). Monitoring of understanding: An investigation of good and poor readers' awareness of induced miscomprehension of text. *Journal of Reading Behavior, 12,* 5–63.

Glenberg, A.M., Wilkinson, A.C., & Epstein, W. (1982). The illusion of knowing: Failure in the self-assessment of comprehension. *Memory & Cognition, 10,* 597–602.

Graesser, A. C., & Kreuz, R. J. (1993). A theory of inference generation during text comprehension. *Discourse Processes, 16,* 146–60.

Graesser, A. C., Singer, M., & Trabasso, T. (1994). Constructing inferences during narrative text comprehension. *Psychological Review, 101,* 371–95.

Hacker, D. J. (1997). Comprehension monitoring of written discourse across early-to-middle adolescence. *Reading and Writing, 9,* 207–40.

Harcourt Assessment. (1996). *Stanford 9.* San Antonio, TX: Author.

Hart, L. A. (2005). *A training study using an artificial orthography: Effects of reading experience, lexical quality, and text comprehension in L1 and L2* (Unpublished doctoral dissertation). University of Pittsburgh, Pittsburgh, PA.

Keenan, J. M., Betjemann, R. S., & Olson, R. K. (2008). Reading comprehension tests vary in the skills they assess: Differential dependence on decoding and oral comprehension. *Scientific Studies of Reading, 12,* 281–300.

Kintsch, W., & Rawson, K. A. (2005). Comprehension. In M. J. Snowling & C. Hulme (Eds.), *The science of reading: A handbook* (pp. 209–26). Oxford: Blackwell.

Kletzien, S. B. (1991). Strategy use by good and poor comprehenders reading expository text of differing levels. *Reading Research Quarterly, 26,* 67-86.

Landi, N. (2010). An examination of the relationship between reading comprehension, higher-level and lower-level reading sub-skills in adults. *Reading and Writing, 23,* 701–17.

Landi, N., & Perfetti, C. A. (2007). An electrophysiological investigation of semantic and phonological processing in skilled and less-skilled comprehenders. *Brain and Language, 102,* 30–45.

McKoon, G., & Ratcliff, R. (1992). Inference during reading. *Psychological Review, 99,* 440–46.

Muter, V., Hulme, C., Snowling, M., & Stevenson, J. (2004). Phonemes, rimes, vocabulary, and grammatical skills as foundations of early reading development: Evidence from a longitudinal study. *Developmental Psychology, 40,* 665–81.

Nagy, W. E. & Herman, P. A. (1987). Breadth and depth of vocabulary knowledge: Implications for acquisition and instruction. In M. G. McKeown & M. E. Curtis (Eds.), *The nature of vocabulary acquisition* (pp. 19–35). Hillsdale, NJ: Lawrence Erlbaum Associates.

Nagy, W. E., & Scott, J. A. (2000). Vocabulary processes. In M. Kamil, P. Mosenthal, P. D. Pearson, & R. Barr (Eds.), *Handbook of reading research* (Vol. III, pp. 269–84). New York: Longman.

Nation, K., & Snowling, M. J. (1999). Developmental differences in sensitivity to semantic relations among good and poor comprehenders: evidence from semantic priming. *Cognition, 70,* B1–B13.

National Reading Panel. (2000). *Report of the National Reading Panel. Teaching children to read: An evidence-based assessment of the scientific research literature on reading and its implications for reading instruction* (NIH Publication No. 00-4769). Washington, D.C.: U.S. Government Printing Office.

Oakhill, J. (1984). Inferential and memory skills in children's comprehension of stories. *British Journal of Educational Psychology, 54,* 31–39.

Oakhill, J., Hartt, J., & Samols, D. (2005). Levels of comprehension monitoring and working memory in good and poor comprehenders. *Reading and Writing, 18,* 657–86.

Olshavsky, J. E. (1977). Reading as problem solving: An investigation of strategies. *Reading Research Quarterly, 12,* 654–74.

Otero, J., & Kintsch, W. (1992). Failures to detect contradictions in a text: What readers believe versus what they read. *Psychological Science, 3,* 229–35.

Ouellette, G. P. (2006). What's meaning got to do with it: The role of vocabulary in word reading and reading comprehension. *Journal of Educational Psychology, 98,* 554–66.

Perfetti, C. (1985). *Reading ability.* New York: Oxford Press.

———. (2007). Reading ability: Lexical quality to comprehension. *Scientific Studies of Reading, 11,* 357–83.

Perfetti, C. A., & Hart, L. (2001). The lexical bases of comprehension skill. In D. Gorfien (Ed.), *On the consequences of meaning selection* (pp. 67–86). Washington, D.C.: American Psychological Association.

Sabatini, J. P. (2002). Efficiency in word reading of adults: Ability group comparisons. *Scientific Studies of Reading, 6,* 267–98.

———. (2003). Word reading processes in adult learners. In E. M. H. Assink & D. Sandra (Eds.), *Reading complex words: Cross-language studies* (pp. 265–94). London: Kluwer Academic.

Storch, S. A., & Whitehurst, G. J. (2002). Oral language and code-related precursors to reading: evidence from a longitudinal structural model. *Developmental Psychology, 38,* 934–47.

Tannenbaum, K. R., Torgesen, J. K., & Wagner, R. K. (2006). Relationships between word knowledge and reading comprehension in third-grade children. *Scientific Studies of Reading, 10,* 381–98.

Trabasso, T., & Suh, S. (1993). Understanding text: Achieving explanatory coherence through on-line inferences and mental operations in working memory. *Discourse Processes, 16,* 3–34.

van den Broek, P. (2012). Individual and developmental differences in reading comprehension: Assessing cognitive processes and outcomes. In J. P. Sabatini, E. Albro, & T. O'Reilly (Eds.), *Measuring Up: Advances in how we assess reading ability* (pp. 39–58). Lanham, MD: Rowman & Littlefield Education.

van den Broek, P., Risden, K., & Husebye-Hartmann, E. (1995). The role of readers' standards for coherence in the generation of inferences during reading. In R.F. Lorch, Jr. & E. J. O'Brien (Eds.), *Standards of coherence in reading* (pp. 353–73). New York: Routledge.

van der Schoot, M., Vasbinder, A. L., Horsley, T. M., Reijntjes, A., & van Lieshout, E. C. D. M. (2009). Lexical ambiguity resolution in good and poor comprehenders: An eye fixation and self-paced reading study in primary school children. *Journal of Educational Psychology, 101,* 21–36.

Van Dijk, T. A., & Kintsch, W. (1983). *Strategies of discourse comprehension.* New York: Academic Press.

Vosniadou, S., Pearson, P. D., & Rogers, T. (1988). What causes children's failures to detect inconsistencies in texts? Representation versus comparison difficulties. *Journal of Educational Psychology, 80,* 27–39.

Wagner, R. (2005, April). *Causal relations between vocabulary development and reading comprehension.* Paper presented at the Meeting of the American Educational Research Association, Toronto.

Williams, K. T. (2007). *Expressive Vocabulary Test.* Circle Pines, MN: American Guidance Service.

Wilson, V. L., & Rupley, W. H. (1997). A structural equation model for reading comprehension based on background, phonemic, and strategy knowledge. *Scientific Studies of Reading, 1,* 45–63.

Woodcock, R. W. (1998). *Woodcock Reading Mastery Tests-Revised.* Circle Pines, MN: American Guidance Services.

Yang, C. L., Perfetti, C. A., & Schmalhofer, F. (2005). Less skilled comprehenders' ERPs show sluggish word-to-text integration processes. *Written Language & Literacy, 8,* 233–57.

———. (2007). Event-related potential indicators of text integration across sentence boundaries. *Journal of Experimental Psychology-Learning Memory and Cognition, 33,* 55–89.

Yuill, N., & Oakhill, J. (1991). *Children's problems in text comprehension.* Cambridge, UK: Cambridge University Press.

Zwaan, R. A., & Radvansky, G. A. (1998). Situation models in language comprehension and memory. *Psychological Bulletin, 123,* 162–85.

NOTES

1. Suzanne Adlof is a post-doctoral fellow supported through a Post-doctoral Research Training Fellowship in the Education Sciences awarded by IES [R305B050022] to Charles Perfetti, whose research is supported by NICHD (Child Development and Behavior Branch) award 1R01HD058566-01A1. The content of the chapter also was shaped by work supported by an earlier research award from IES to the first author [R305G020006].

2. Most studies of SCD readers use word reading accuracy for matching SCD readers with controls (but see Adlof, 2010). Theoretically, speed beyond accuracy is an indicator of word processing efficiency, so naming times or other speed measures are desirable to have a fuller picture of word level skills. Naming speed may have its effect on reading comprehension mainly indirectly through oral language skill, as suggested by the results of Adlof, Catts, & Little (2006).

3. ERPs are shifts in electrical activity in the brain that are time-locked to an event, such as the presentation of a stimulus in an experiment. Shifts in voltage are measured using electroencephalogram (EEG) technology. ERPs are particularly useful for studying cognitive processes because they do not require an external response and because of their excellent temporal resolution. ERP components are frequently described in terms of their polarity (i.e., positive or negative), as well as their latency in milliseconds after the stimulus onset. Thus, a P200 reflects a positive shift in voltage at approximately 200 milliseconds after the stimulus onset.

Chapter Two

Psychological Models of Reading Comprehension and Their Implications for Assessment

Walter Kintsch

I believe evaluation of the psychological processes involved in reading comprehension must be a key component of comprehension assessment. This is not how comprehension assessment currently works. Typically, comprehension is assessed by giving students a short text to read and asking a small number of questions. The questions are selected to discriminate between good and poor readers as otherwise determined. The questions are not designed with comprehension theory in mind and are scored to yield a single index of comprehension.

In contrast, when comprehension is assessed in the laboratory in a psychological experiment, a variety of methods are used, questions are targeted at specific aspects of comprehension, and the different component processes of comprehension are evaluated separately. I shall describe the procedures used in a laboratory setting and discuss their advantages, with the goal of outlining the properties of a well-designed comprehension test.

I am not claiming that comprehension assessment in schools should become a domain of cognitive science. It is my belief that the problem with current practices is that they are dominated by psychometric considerations and neglect cognitive issues as well as the concerns and needs of other stakeholders in comprehension assessment. What is needed in comprehension assessment is a coordinated approach involving psychometricians, cognitive scientists, and experts in reading development and subject matter learning.

For clarity and specificity, I shall frame my discussion in terms of the model of comprehension of Kintsch (1998), which shares its principal features with other models of comprehension (for reviews, see Graesser, 2007; Zwaan & Singer, 2003). The goal of the construction-integration model of Kintsch (1998), which grew out of the earlier work of Kintsch & van Dijk (1978), van Dijk & Kintsch (1983), and Kintsch (1988), is to describe the psychological processes involved in reading a text and in responding to the text in some way (recalling it, answering questions about it, learning from it). The model neglects the decoding and word recognition process, i.e., how the printed symbols on the page are turned into words and language.

Much of the research on reading acquisition in early grades has been concerned with this important and crucial process, and word identification is reasonably well understood today, as are its implications for instruction and assessment. For the purposes of this chapter, we will deal with more or less fluent word readers and focus on what happens once the words have been recognized.

Suppose a reader has encoded a sentence in a text he or she is reading.[1] To comprehend it, he or she must link it up with information presented earlier in the text as well as with relevant prior knowledge. Furthermore, the sentence that is being processed in working memory must be stored in some more permanent form so it becomes available for integration with the sentences in the text yet to be read.

After reading the whole text, the reader has a representation of the meaning of the text in long-term memory. This representation is patched together from the different processing cycles involved and linked in various ways to his or her prior knowledge and relevant personal experiences. This representation must support a variety of text-related behaviors: sentence recognition; text recall and summarization; recognition of main ideas; recognition of text structure and genre; answering of questions about the text, including inferences requiring prior knowledge; use of the information in problem solving; and knowledge updating. It is useful for theoretical purposes to distinguish several distinct levels within that representation, primarily the surface structure, textbase, and situation model.

The linguistic surface structure is a representation of the actual words and their syntactic relations. Verbatim memory reflects this surface structure. It is usually quickly forgotten (but not necessarily so) and of lesser relevance in our educational system.

The textbase is a symbolic representation of the meaning of the text in terms of propositions and their interrelationship. The term "proposition" is used here to represent the intuitive notion of idea unit. Forming a textbase is the first step in the comprehension process considered here. A good textbase is representative of the meaning of the text and its structure.

The situation model integrates portions of the textbase with the reader's prior knowledge and reading goals. Typically, it selects those aspects of the textbase that are relevant to reading goals and links them to the existing knowledge base, which is thereby modified and expanded. Because individual reading goals and knowledge bases differ, the exact nature of the situation model that a reader forms is sometimes hard to anticipate. The situation model is multimodal, combining symbolic representations with sensory imagery, action representations, and emotional markers. Situation models are also cumulative: New knowledge from the text being read is integrated with prior knowledge. Hence, learning from text can be considered a process of situation model updating.

Comprehension always requires knowledge and skills. To form a textbase, one needs knowledge of a language, including vocabulary and grammar, as well as its conventions of discourse. For the purposes of this chapter, we will deal with readers who have adequate language and discourse skills and knowledge, acquired over many years of listening and reading.

To form a situation model, additional knowledge is usually required: knowledge about the domain of the text. Situation models involve knowledge updating, yet to construct a situation model, relevant domain knowledge is often needed to fill in gaps in the text. Just as bridging inferences are required to form a coherent textbase, world knowledge is often needed to form an adequate situation model.

Even the most experienced reader cannot comprehend a technical text outside his or her domain of expertise. I once demonstrated that I could write an acceptable summary of an abstruse physics text purely on the basis of my general language knowledge, but I had no idea what that text was about. Physicists would have understood that text in a very different way. Many of the words and propositions in the text would have resonated with the physicists' prior knowledge, and whatever new information the text contained would have been automatically linked to an already existing situation model.

One needs to know something to learn something new. For the expert, that is an automatic process: The text propositions held in working memory automatically are linked with the reader's knowledge via retrieval structures formed through extensive practice and wide reading in the individual's domain of expertise (Ericsson & Kintsch, 1995). It takes about ten years of practice to become an expert (Simon, 1969), but once all the necessary knowledge is acquired, it will automatically and easily support text comprehension in a person's domain of expertise.

For students who read various kinds of technical text on the way to becoming an expert, the demands of comprehension are very different. They cannot rely on the automatic activation of relevant knowledge; for them, comprehension becomes an effortful, strategic process. They must consciously search their memory for relevant knowledge, continuously monitor their level of comprehension, and actively try to construct a situation model. That is hard work, and readers often like to get by without it, which is why shallow, superficial comprehension is such a problem in schools. Students can regurgitate what the teacher or the book said, but they lack deep understanding. They may have constructed a textbase representation, but they failed to construct a new situation model or update an already existing knowledge structure.

Consequently, they have learned nothing. An important task for educators is to get students to do that hard work. This involves motivating them, giving them a purpose to engage in the effort. At the same time, we need to schedule students' learning materials in such a way that they remain within the students' zone of proximal learning, allowing them to always have sufficient prior knowledge to understand what they read, albeit with effort.

Stories are one kind of text where most adults and many students have expertise, which makes them easy to comprehend. Stories are about human actions, the motivations behind them, and outcomes; people have excellent situation models for such things, honed through many years of living in a society. Hence the popularity of narratives, in real life as well as in the laboratory: everybody can understand them, everybody is an expert, and what people do and why is often quite interesting. Even very young children are able to represent goals and actions of individuals in simple stories with remarkable sophistication. Character development in literature, however, is a more demanding task requiring deeper knowledge, maturity, and frequently effortful analysis.

Table 2.1 shows how knowledge and reading skills interact (see also Coté, Goldman, & Saul, 1998). If reading skills and domain knowledge are high, the result is automatic, expert comprehension. If reading skills and domain knowledge are low, comprehension is impaired. In school, it is often the case that we are dealing with students with strong reading skills who are supposed to learn from what they read, that is, they are able to read texts in an unfamiliar domain.

Comprehension here is not automatic, it requires effort and good reading strategies. Here is where comprehension instruction can really help. The last situation in Table 2.1 is rarely encountered but is of considerable theoretical interest: weak readers who are experts in a domain and outperform skilled readers who lack such expertise. The weak readers' expert ability to form a situation model (e.g., what happened in a soccer game) more than compensates for their lack of reading skills. Thus, one way to help poor readers

Table 2.1. The interaction between reading skills and domain knowledge

	Weak Reading Skills	*Strong Reading Skills*
Low Knowledge	*poor comprehension*	*effortful comprehension*
High Knowledge	*good comprehension in special domain*	*automatic comprehension*

with low knowledge is to build up their knowledge base, allowing them to compensate for their lack of reading skills.

I have focused here on just two aspects of comprehension theory: the mental representation of texts in terms of textbase and situation model, and the contrast between the automatic comprehension of domain experts and the resource-demanding comprehension of novices for complex expository texts. Next, I shall describe a few selected experiments that illustrate the kind of problems that comprehension researchers have investigated in the laboratory and the methods used to assess comprehension.

TEXTBASES

While the textbase-situation model distinction is useful, it should be noted that these are not stages of processing but are simultaneous and interdependent. Indeed, some authors (e.g., Sanford & Garrod, 1989) have correctly argued that readers often jump directly to the situation model without bothering about a propositional textbase. Especially for school learning, however, basing a situation model on a representative textbase is very important. Students must learn that not everything goes, that they really need to find out just what the text says. Hence, assessing the reader's comprehension at the level of the textbase cannot be neglected (e.g., Resnick & Hamilton, 2009).

I briefly sketch some of the issues in textbase formation that have been studied in the laboratory, as well as the methods used to do so. Most of these methods will not be feasible for standardized testing, but I want to illustrate the richness and variety of laboratory work in this area.

I am neglecting word identification and vocabulary, not because they are unimportant, but because that literature is widely known. Word identification problems interact with comprehension problems, however, because poor decoders may not have enough cognitive resources to devote to comprehension (Sweller, 1988; see also Perfetti and Adolf, 2012). Similarly, second-language readers often have to spend so much of their mental resources on *translation* that they are unable to construct an adequate situation model, hence failing to understand what they have so laboriously read.

Ratcliff and McKoon's 1978 study provides evidence for the psychological reality of idea units/propositions. Subjects read multiple-proposition sentences and were later given a word recognition test: a sequence of words to which they responded yes or no, depending on whether that word had been seen before. In such experiments, yes responses are faster when a word from the same sentence precedes the test word. Importantly, reaction times are even faster when a word is not only from the same sentence, but the same proposition also precedes the test word. Having just accessed a mental unit—a proposition—facilitates recognition of elements of that proposition.

But not all propositions are equal: some, called *macro-propositions*, play an important role in the structure of the text, expressing the main points of the text. Others are subordinated in that structure, expressing textual details (*micro-propositions*). Recognition priming for macro-propositions is much stronger than for micro-propositions (Guindon & Kintsch, 1984).

When building connections across propositions, readers depend upon the linguistic structures of the text. One linguistic structure widely studied in the laboratory is *referent identification*, or *anaphora*. Languages have many ways to identify a discourse referent, ranging from zero-anaphora to pronouns to full noun phrases. These are not used interchangeably but have important signaling functions. Good readers are sensitive to these signals: when a referent is introduced with "this," it is deemed more important than when introduced with merely "a."

In an experiment by Gernsbacher and Schroyer (1989), subjects were given a sentence fragment and asked to complete it. When a discourse object was introduced with "this" (as in, *"There was this guy in my class last semester . . ."*), the continuations that readers generated contained almost twice as many references to the discourse object than when it was introduced with "a" (*"There was a guy in my class last semester..."*).

Similarly, the sort of anaphora used depends on the coherence of two sentences. When the sentences are coherent, people use a pronoun or nothing at all, but when they are incoherent, people use a full noun phrase to avoid confusion (Fletcher, 1984). Thus we get *"Pete intended to go bowling last night. HE broke his leg,"* but *"Sam intended to go bowling with Pete last night. PETE broke his leg."*

The topic involved in textbase formation that has received the most attention in laboratory studies is that of *inference*. There is no way I can review here the literature on this complex subject, but a few examples will suffice to illustrate the richness of the work in this area.

First, regarding the term inference, we are not (usually) talking about logical inferences. Discourse inferences are either knowledge based (a sentence with the word *car* is coherent with a sentence with the word *door*, because we know that a door is a part of car) or constructed (if *Peter is taller than John*, and *Mary is taller than Peter,* the inference that *Mary is taller than John* is generated). Furthermore, when inferences are in a familiar domain, inference formation is automatic, as in the examples above. But in unfamiliar domains, inference formation is a controlled, resource-demanding process, as shown in Table 2.2.

But how all these factors interact in a discourse context is full of wrinkles and subtleties. Consider a paragraph from one of our experiments that re-

Table 2.2. Inference types

	Retrieval	Generation
Automatic	familiar bridging inferences "The car stopped. The driver opened the door" à car door	familiar transitive inferences "Peter is taller than John. Mary is taller than Peter" à "Mary is taller than John"
Controlled	unfamiliar bridging inferences "Connors used Kevlar sails because he expected little wind" à "Kevlar sails are advantageous when the weather is calm"	logical inferences "If today is Tuesday, then I will go to work. Today is Tuesday." à "Therefore, I will go to work."

quired a simple, highly familiar causal inference (e.g., "*It rained last night. The streets are wet.*"). In one case the inference was spelled out in a separate sentence; in the other case it was left implicit. There was no difference in the time subjects took to read these paragraphs, but when they were given the inference sentence to verify, they needed extra time to verify the sentence when it was implicit (Kintsch & Keenan, 1973). This finding indicates that readers did not make the inference when reading, but only when asked to do so on the test.

But everything is different when we vary this experiment just a little bit: when the inference is left implicit, but we signal that something is missing by adding a sentence connective (such as "but" or "therefore"). In this case, readers make the inference at the time of reading (taking longer to read) but are equally fast at verification, whether they read the explicit or implicit text (Noordman & Vonk, 1992).

Almost everything matters in inference generation, especially the time course. When a word is read in a discourse context, it takes about 300 milliseconds (ms) for its meaning to become fixed. Simple automatic inferences (e.g., topic inferences, causal inferences) take longer, from about 400 ms to 750 ms (Long, Oppy, & Seely, 1994; Magliano, Baggett, Johnson, & Graesser, 1993; Till, Mross & Kintsch, 1988).

But whether such inferences are made at all depends on a variety of factors. If you ask readers to make an inference, there is almost no limit to what they can generate (Graesser, 1981). On the other hand, if you leave it to the readers to make inferences or not, they can be stingy about it, leading McKoon & Ratcliff (1992) to espouse the minimalist hypothesis: readers form only those inferences that are absolutely necessary for the coherence of the textbase.

In actuality, readers fluctuate between these extremes, depending on conditions (Graesser, Singer, & Trabasso, 1994). In school settings, the problem is usually to get students to read actively, that is, to spend the additional mental effort needed to form an accurate situation model and to make the inferences necessary for a coherent textbase.

SITUATION MODELS

The textbase is a verbal, linguistic construction. The situation model integrates the linguistic structure with world knowledge. It explains why the second set of sentences below is unacceptable (after Sanford & Garrod, 1989):

a) *Harry put the wallpaper on the table. Then he put his mug of coffee on the paper.*
b) *Harry put the wallpaper on the wall. Then he put his mug of coffee on the paper.*

Just what sort of situation model readers will form depends on their reading goals as well as the peculiarities of their prior knowledge. A few examples will serve to illustrate the variety of situation models in response to different types of text.

Narratives have a conventional structure that is described by *story grammar*. Story grammars consist of a series of episodes linked primarily by causal and temporal relations: goals to actions, actions to outcomes, etc. The situation model that readers form is a causal network of episodes (Trabasso & Suh, 1993; van den Broek, 1990). Human data on story understanding (recall, explanation, summarization) are well accounted for by such networks, and mapping techniques have been developed to document such story structures.

For instance, story structure may have a node for a goal proposition that is directly linked to several other story episodes. Trabasso and Suh (1993) found that a reference to the goal node is three times as likely in directly linked episodes as in the rest of the story in subjects' recall—evidence that recall is guided by the links that the story grammar postulates.

The construction of a situation model requires *inference processes*. We have already mentioned bridging inferences that play a role in the coherence of the textbase, and causal inferences, as in the situation models for the narratives above. Singer (1990) provides an example of a bridging inference that proficient readers routinely make while reading:

The spy threw the report into the fire. The ashes floated up the chimney.

The second sentence is not coherent unless the reader makes the inference that the report burned to ashes. Various experimental methods, such as cued recall, response times, and speeded judgment of single words have been used to determine whether readers form such inferences.

Another type of inference, an elaborative inference, is not strictly required for the coherence of the text. The sentence pair below does not lack coherence (*he* refers to *spy*) and the inference that the report burned is elective:

The spy threw the report into the fire. Then he called the airline.

However, elaborative inferences are often important in the formation of the situation model. Most situation models for stories require some elaboration, beyond mere bridging inferences—for example, inferences about character goals, motives, and emotional states. Good comprehenders tend to make the elaborative inferences that a text invites; poor readers fail to do so, or, in some cases, elaborate wildly beyond what the text supports.

Some texts require *spatial* situation models. These can be simple mental images that are formed automatically, as in the classic paper by Bransford, Barclay, and Franks, 1972. Bransford et al. gave subjects sentence pairs to read such as:

a) Three turtles rested on a floating log and a fish swam beneath them.
b) Three turtles rested on a floating log and a fish swam beneath it.

The situation model for both sentences, a mental image of the turtles on the log with the fish underneath, is the same. Consequently, subjects could not tell them apart on a recognition test. On the other hand, when the mental image was different, recognition confusions were rare:

a) Three turtles rested beside a floating log and a fish swam beneath them.
b) Three turtles rested beside a floating log and a fish swam beneath it.

Of course, not all spatial inferences are automatic. Sometimes complex constructions are involved that require substantial mental effort. Perrig and Kintsch (1985) gave readers a description of the spatial layout of a fictitious town and then tested their memory either with sentences from the text they had read, or with sentences that could be inferred from the text. While their memory for what they had read was good, they had not formed a situation model. Consequently, their performance on inference tests was near zero. However, different results were obtained when the text was simplified and readers were given plenty of time to study it. In that case, readers were able to form a good situation model, as indicated by their performance on the inference tests.

Interestingly, for readers who managed to form a spatial situation model, the nature of that model determined how well they could find their way around town in response to specific instructions. The situation model for some readers was a mental map, for others a route description. People who rely on a mental map navigated well when given an instruction like, "Turn east on 34th Street," but not with, "Turn left after the church." It was just the opposite for the route people (Perrig & Kintsch, 1985).

Both had formed a spatial situation model, but the exact details of that model influenced their ability to find their way around the town. Thus, when readers were given instructions in the same form as their situation model, they performed well, but when the instructions did not conform to the way they had represented the town, they made numerous errors.

In the studies just mentioned, a question-answering methodology was used. There are various other techniques that can be used to assess the quality of readers' situation models (and comprehension). For instance, a good way to find out how much readers learn from a text describing the functioning of the heart and circulatory system is to have them draw a diagram of how they think the system works before and after reading. The diagrams can be classi- fied into a few types (e.g., no loop, single loop, two forms of double loop—as seen in Figure 2.1), and the number of readers who move from a primitive type to a more accurate type gives a good estimate of the effectiveness of the text (Butcher, 2006).

Not all texts lend themselves to drawing diagrams, so Butcher used a second method that turned out to be equally informative. She classified the self-explanations of her readers and noted which texts gave rise to low-level self-explanations (e.g., paraphrases) and which produced more sophisticated self-explanations (e.g., integrative inferences). The texts that yielded the most elaborate self-explanations were the ones from which readers learned most.

I have presented the research on textbase and situation model construction with just a few examples, but with some detail about their methodology, to demonstrate the many different aspects of comprehension and the various methods used for investigating them in the laboratory. Comprehension as- sessment in school settings must somehow find a way to deal with that com- plexity. It obviously cannot be done with the laboratory methods described above, but suitable alternatives must be found, especially for distinguishing between textbase and situation model understanding in assessment, to which I turn now.

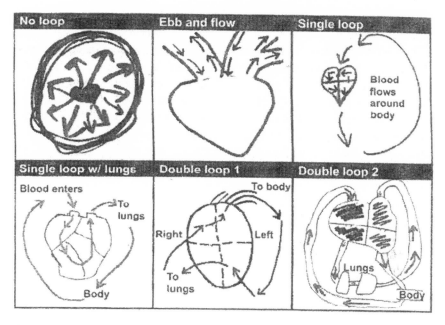

Figure 2.1. Situation models for a text on the circulatory system can be evaluated by drawing a diagram pre- and post reading.

TEXTBASE AND THE SITUATION MODEL: DIFFERENCES IN ASSESSMENT

Given the different requirements for the construction of the textbase and the situation model, it should be no surprise that comprehension assessment is complex and that the results depend on a number of factors. What matters most is the level of comprehension that is assessed—the textbase or the situation model—and the background knowledge of the readers, whether they are novices relying on resource-demanding strategic processes or akin to experts relying on efficient retrieval structures. Oversimplifying only somewhat, readers can be treated as domain experts when reading familiar texts, such as simple stories, but are domain novices with respect to many other texts they encounter in school, such as science texts.

There are a number of studies that demonstrate the importance of the textbase-situation model distinction for assessment. In the original study exploring this distinction (McNamara, E. Kintsch, Songer, & W. Kintsch, 1996), students studied a fairly long text describing heart disease. Two forms of the text were produced. One was as coherent, explicit, and well-written as we could make it. The other was intentionally made difficult: sentence connectives were missing, referents were ambiguous, and the macrostructure of the text was poorly signaled. But the content of the two texts was the same.

Two groups of subjects were used: one with high prior knowledge about the heart, the other with low knowledge. When comprehension was measured with a memory task that asked them to recall a particular section of the text or by answering text-based questions, the coherent, well-written text yielded better results than the poorly written text for both high- and low-knowledge subjects. High-knowledge subjects recalled more than low-knowledge subjects.

When comprehension was measured by problem-solving questions or a conceptual sorting task, however, the results were quite different: Low-knowledge subjects performed better with the well-written text (their performance was almost at zero with the difficult text), but high-knowledge subjects actually did better when they had read the difficult text than when they had read the easy text.

By giving subjects a difficult text to read, we forced them into active processing. They had to work hard to figure out what the text meant and in the process formed a good situation model that allowed them to answer the inference questions. But that was possible only for the subjects who had sufficient prior knowledge to make the required bridging inferences to sort out the coherence problems with the text. The low-knowledge subjects were simply lost. On the other hand, when the high-knowledge subjects read the well-written text, they understood it easily, but at a superficial level: They never bothered to construct a good situation model but were satisfied with their easy understanding.

This study, which has been extended and replicated in various ways by several authors, exemplifies the problem of comprehension assessment. Comprehension is not a unitary process that can be measured with a single score. At minimum, it requires a distinction between superficial and deep comprehension—comprehension at the level of the textbase versus the level of the situation model.

A recent study investigated individual differences in comprehension at the levels of the textbase and the situation model (Mulligan, 2006). College students read six, fairly long, expository texts. The length is significant, because short texts do not make sufficient organizational demands and hence are unsuitable to investigate the full range of comprehension processes (Rawson & Kintsch, 2005).

For each text, we asked the subjects to recall it and answer an inference question. The inference question was designed to require several pieces of information from the text to be integrated in order to yield the expected inference. Inference questions were carefully constructed so they could not be answered correctly on the basis of general knowledge without using the information from the text (Keenan & Betjemann, 2006). Answers to inference questions were of paragraph length.

For each subject, we plotted average memory performance versus average inference performance. As expected, memory scores were higher than inference scores and the two were significantly correlated ($r = .56$). However, we also found that memory sets an upper bound for inference scores. Good memory allows good inferencing but does not guarantee it. Indeed, subjects who received a high memory score (a grade of A or B) had inference scores ranging from F to B+.

From an assessment standpoint, this finding seems important: inferencing was more than two standard deviations below what one would expect on the basis of their memory performance for about one in seven readers. A student who does poorly on the inference questions but well on the memory questions is very different from one who does poorly, both in terms of the kind of remediation and instruction needed.

Another way of looking at the Mulligan (2006) data is through a confirmatory factor analysis. A one-factor model did not fit the data, but a two-factor model fit well. The memory factor accounted for more of the variance than the inference factor, and the two were highly correlated, but the inference factor made an independent, statistically significant—and, I believe—educationally significant contribution.

A direct link between laboratory results such as the ones described here and educational practices was established in a study by Rapp, van den Broek, McMaster, Kendeou, and Espin (2007). Using eye-tracking methods and think-aloud protocols, the authors distinguished between two kinds of struggling readers at three grade levels. In one subgroup, comprehension failures occurred because readers restricted their focus to the current text, trying to construct a textbase but failing to form a situation model. In a second subgroup, however, which was indistinguishable from the first in terms of standard performance measures, readers attempted to build situation models but were unsuccessful, mostly because they invoked inappropriate background knowledge. Thus, poor comprehension performance may have different causes, requiring different types of instructional interventions. The task for comprehension assessment is to reliably identify these causes.

IMPLICATIONS FOR ASSESSMENT

Researchers familiar with the comprehension literature are undoubtedly aware there is so much more that could be discussed here, so many significant issues that have not been addressed. All I can do here is illustrate the richness and complexity of the field with the purpose of eliciting help from the psychometricians, reading specialists, and subject matter experts, because we strongly need better tests to assess comprehension.

What does all this mean for assessment? An obvious question is whether we should look for a unidimensional measurement of comprehension and text difficulty, or whether a more complex multidimensional test is required. The traditional view is the former. Text difficulty is measured by a single score. Depending on the task, that performance level may vary, e.g., performance would be better on a recall test than an inference test. But in principle, a text with a higher "readability" score should always be harder to recall and more difficult to derive inferences from than a text with a lower score. The situation is similar for the student, who is characterized by some "reading skill" score. The student with the higher score should always perform better than the one with a lower score, irrespective of the task at hand.

The multidimensional view allows for a more complex picture. Some texts may be easy to summarize because they have a clear and well-signaled macrostructure, but they may not support inferences well because too much is left unsaid. Another text may be hard to recall because it contains a lot of confusing detail, but it is easily summarized in just a few words and affords some obvious inferences. The student situation is similar: Some students may be good at recall but fail to make appropriate text-supported inferences, as we have seen in the Mulligan (2006) data described above. Others are all-too-ready to make inferences, without bothering to find out exactly which ones are supported by the text.

If we take the multidimensional view of text difficulty and reading skill, some questions arise. What are the educationally relevant dimensions? What needs to be the focus in instruction and assessment, and which aspect of comprehension can safely be neglected because students do not have any serious problem with it? The data reviewed here suggest that the textbase-situation model distinction is certainly relevant, but it is quite likely that finer distinctions need to be made for practical purposes.

The role played by motivation and prior knowledge further complicates the picture. The difficulty of a complex text depends crucially on the prior knowledge of the reader. The soccer fans of Schneider, Körkel, and Weinert (1989), who were poor readers, comprehended stories about soccer games with ease, while expert readers who knew little about the game were confused. Prior knowledge is crucially important in determining text difficulty and comprehension. Furthermore, one of the main "skills" in reading is to use one's prior knowledge to understand the text—something poor readers often fail to do.

Motivation is closely tied to prior knowledge. People are motivated by their interests, and interests depend on a fairly high level of familiarity (though not too high). Thus, comprehension testing with texts that are unfamiliar, out of context and of low interest may miss something.

So what should we assess? Should we look at students' peak performance with texts that are familiar and interesting? Or should we consider their skill with unfamiliar texts? Or should we try to determine how well they are able to use knowledge acquired in one text for comprehending a novel text? These are questions that must be answered, not by considering the cognitive literature on comprehension alone, but through the joint efforts of all stakeholders in comprehension assessment.

A further consideration concerns the goals of assessment, because formative and summative assessment makes different demands. In tutoring, the goal of assessment is to provide on-line help to a reader with a particular text. To minimize interruptions, this is typically done through questions at the end of short sections of the text. If an answer is acceptable, reading continues; if not, further probing, explanation, and re-reading might be necessary. The questions are designed to probe various aspects of the textbase and situation model formation, as well as relevant background knowledge.

One dimension along which questions vary is specificity. Some are generic prompts to summarize; some are text-specific macro-statements or explanations, e.g. of a causal chain (why? how?); some may be text-specific fact questions (what? when? where? who?). The second dimension of variation is the level of representation addressed. Questions can refer to the textbase (fact-finding questions); the macrostructure of the textbase (summarization); or to the situation model (simple inferences, knowledge-based inferences, integrative inferences, interpretation, distinguishing fact from claim, prediction, and speculation).

In standardized testing, the goals are different, and while the same kind of questions can be used, they must be aggregated into a set of scores that characterize an individual's comprehension performance (e.g., memory and inference scores).

Better comprehension tests that really assess deep comprehension are essential. Instructional programs that foster deep comprehension cannot get widespread acceptance as long as we evaluate them with tests that do not measure what students learn in those programs. The need has been widely recognized (e.g., Shepard, 2000). Now, something needs to be done about it.

REFERENCES

Bransford, J. D., Barclay, J. R., & Franks, J. J. (1972). Sentence memory: A constructive versus interpretive approach. *Cognitive Psychology, 3*, 193–209.

Butcher, K. R. (2006). Learning from text with diagrams: Promoting mental model development and inference generation. *Journal of Educational Psychology, 98,* 182–97.

Coté, N., Goldman, S. R., & Saul, E. U. (1998). Students making sense of informational text: Relations between processing and representation. *Discourse Processes, 25,* 1–53.

Ericsson, K. A., & Kintsch, W. (1995). Long-term working memory. *Psychological Review, 102,* 211–45.

Fletcher, C. R. (1984). Markedness and topic continuity in discourse processing. *Journal of Verbal Learning and Verbal Behavior, 23,* 487–93.

Gernsbacher, M. A., & Shroyer, S. (1989). The cataphoric use of the indefinite this in spoken narratives. *Memory & Cognition, 17,* 538–40.

Graesser, A. C. (1981). *Prose comprehension beyond the word.* New York: Springer.

———. (2007). An introduction to strategic reading comprehension. In D. S. McNamara (Ed.), *Reading comprehension strategies* (pp. 3–26). Mahwah, NJ: Lawrence Erlbaum Associates.

Graesser, A. C., Singer, M., & Trabasso, T. (1994). Constructing inferences during narrative text comprehension. *Psychological Review, 101,* 375–95.

Guindon, R., & Kintsch, W. (1984). Priming macropropositions: Evidence for the primacy of macropropositions in memory. *Journal of Verbal Learning and Verbal Behavior, 23,* 508–18.

Keenan, J. M., & Betjeman, R. S. (2006). Comprehending the Gray oral reading test without reading it: Why comprehension tests should not include passage-independent items. *Scientific Studies of Reading, 10,* 363–80.

Kintsch, W. (1988). The use of knowledge in discourse processing: A construction-integration model. *Psychological Review, 95,* 163–82.

———. (1998). *Comprehension: A paradigm for cognition.* New York: Cambridge University Press.

Kintsch, W., & Keenan, J. M. (1973). Reading rate and retention as a function of the number of propositions in the base structure of sentences. *Cognitive Psychology, 5,* 257–79.

Kintsch, W., & van Dijk, T. A. (1978). Towards a model of text comprehension and production. *Psychological Review, 85,* 363–94.

Long, D. L., Oppy, B. J., & Seely, M. R. (1994). Individual differences in the time course of differential processing. *Journal of Experimental Psychology: Learning, Memory, and Cognition, 20,* 1456–470.

Magliano, J. P., Baggett, W. B., Johnson, B. K., & Graesser, A. C. (1993). The time course of generating causal antecedent and causal consequence inferences. *Discourse Processes, 16,* 35–53.

McKoon, G., & Ratcliff, R. (1992). Inference during reading. *Psychological Review, 99,* 440–66.

McNamara, D. S., Kintsch, E., Songer, N., & Kintsch, W. (1996). Are good texts always better? Interactions of text coherence, background knowledge, and levels of understanding in learning from text. *Cognition and Instruction, 14,* 1–43.

Mulligan, E. J. (2006). *Assessment of individual differences in the components of comprehension skill* (Unpublished doctoral dissertation). University of Colorado, Boulder, CO.

Noordman, L. G. M., & Vonk, W. (1992). Readers' knowledge and the control of inferences in reading. *Language and Cognitive Processes, 7,* 373–91.

Perrig, W., & Kintsch, W. (1985). Propositional and situational representations of text. *Journal of Memory and Language, 24,* 503–18.

Rapp, D. N., van den Broek, P., McMaster, K. L., Kendeou, P., & Espin, C. A. (2007). Higher-order comprehension processes in struggling readers: A perspective for research and intervention. *Scientific Studies of Reading, 11,* 289–312.

Ratcliff, R., & McKoon, G. (1978). Priming in item recognition: Evidence for the propositional structure of sentences. *Journal of Verbal Learning and Verbal Behavior, 17,* 403–18.

Rawson, K. A., & Kintsch, W. (2005). Rereading effects depend upon time of test. *Journal of Educational Psychology, 97,* 70–80.

Resnick, L. B., & Hamilton, S. (2009). *Reading and writing grade by grade.* Pittsburgh: University of Pittsburgh and the National Center on Education and the Economy.

Sanford, A. J. and Garrod, S. C. (1989). What, when and how? Questions of immediacy in anaphoric reference resolution. *Language and Cognitive Processes, 4,* 235–62.

Schneider, W., Körkel, J., & Weinert, F. E. (1989). Domain-specific knowledge and memory performance: A comparison of high- and low-aptitude children. *Journal of Educational Psychology, 81,* 306–12.

Simon, H. A. (1969). *The sciences of the artificial.* Cambridge, MA: MIT Press.

Shepard, L. A. (2000) The role of assessment in a learning culture. *Educational Researcher, 29,* 4–14.

Singer, M. (1990). *The psychology of language.* Hillsdale, NJ: Lawrence Erlbaum Associates.

Sweller, J. (1988). Cognitive load during problem solving. *Cognitive Science, 12,* 257–85.

Till, R. E., Mross, E. R., & Kintsch, W. (1988). Time course of priming for associate and inference words in a discourse context. *Memory & Cognition, 16,* 283–98.

Trabasso, T., & Suh, S. Y. (1993). Understanding text: Achieving explanatory coherence through on-line inference and mental operations in working memory. *Discourse Process, 16,* 3–34.

van Dijk, T. A., & Kintsch, W. (1983). *Strategies of discourse comprehension.* New York: Academic Press.

van den Broek, P. W. (1990). Causal inferences in the comprehension of narrative texts. In A. C. Graesser & G. H. Bower (Eds.), *Psychology of learning and motivation: Inferences and text comprehension.* (Vol. 25, pp. 175–94). San Diego: Academic Press.

Zwaan, R., & Singer, M. (2003). Text comprehension. In A. C. Graesser, M. A. Gernsbacher & S. R. Goldman (Eds.), *Handbook of discourse processes* (pp. 83–121). Mahwah, NJ: Lawrence Erlbaum Associates.

NOTE

1. A similar story can be told about listening comprehension, though some of the issues are different, e.g., in dialogue.

Chapter Three

Individual and Developmental Differences in Reading Comprehension: Assessing Cognitive Processes and Outcomes

Paul van den Broek

The ability to read and comprehend texts is essential to school success and, more generally, to successful participation in society. Yet large numbers of students in elementary and secondary school struggle to develop adequate comprehension skills; even among adults, comprehension problems are rampant (National Center for Education Statistics, 2007; Paris, Carpenter, Paris, & Hamilton, 2005; Perie, Grigg, & Donahue, 2005; Verhoeven, Biemond, Gijsel, & Netten, 2007). Central to educational efforts to address these problems is the assessment of reading comprehension and of individual differences in comprehension skill (Ehrlich, 1996; Greenberg, Ehri, & Perin, 1997; Perfetti, Yang, & Schmalhofer, 2008).

To develop effective reading comprehension assessment tools, it is useful to understand what it means to comprehend a text as well as individual and developmental differences in the necessary skills. This chapter reviews research findings on these topics and derives implications for the assessment of reading comprehension.

In conducting this examination, it is important to consider both the *outcomes* of reading comprehension and the *processes* that lead to these comprehension outcomes (van den Broek & White, 2012). Successful reading comprehension involves the construction of a coherent mental representation of both the text and related background knowledge; this representation is the cumulative product of processes that occur moment to moment as the text is read. These processes are the main source of success and failure in comprehension, so their consideration is essential to accurate assessment of reading comprehension as well as developing effective interventions.

Reading comprehension assessment tools may be developed for various purposes. For example, assessments may be designed to determine if individual students meet a particular performance standard, to rank-order

individuals on a relevant dimension, or to diagnose sources of difficulty readers may experience. The specific purpose for a tool determines its characteristics and the requirements it must meet (Pressley & Hilden, 2005; van den
Broek, Kendeou, et al., 2005).

In this chapter, the primary focus will be on assessment with the purpose
of gaining insights into the individual differences in children's comprehension of text and the potential cause(s) of a child's success or failure, but other
purposes for assessment will be discussed briefly.

READING COMPREHENSION: MENTAL REPRESENTATIONS, INFERENCES, AND STANDARDS OF COHERENCE

Reading comprehension has been conceptualized in various ways. It has been
defined, for example, as the ability to remember a text (e.g., Cain, Oakhill, &
Lemmon, 2004; Graesser & Clark, 1985; Trabasso, Secco, & van den Broek,
1984), to extract the main ideas from a text (e.g., Baumann, 1983; Trabasso
& van den Broek, 1985; van den Broek, Lynch, Naslund, Ievers-Landis &
Verduin, 2003; van den Broek & Trabasso, 1986; Williams, 1993), to build
coherence within a text (e.g., Graesser, Singer, & Trabasso, 1994; Kintsch &
van Dijk, 1978; O'Brien, 1995; Stein & Glenn, 1979; van den Broek, Risden,
& Husebye-Hartmann, 1995), and to apply the information in a text (e.g.,
Williams, Stafford, Lauer, Hall, & Pollini, 2009).

These varying definitions show that reading comprehension is not a single
activity nor outcome; rather, it is multifaceted. Individuals can be good comprehenders in different ways. For example, a reader may be a good comprehender by virtue of being highly skilled at extracting the gist from the textual
information. A second reader may be skilled at reiterating the detailed chain
of thoughts and events depicted in the text. A third reader may be strong at
applying the textual information.

Although the definitions of reading comprehension vary, they all share
the notion that an essential aspect of understanding a text is that the reader
constructs a mental representation in which its various parts are connected in
meaningful ways to each other as well as to relevant background knowledge
(Kintsch, 1988; 1998; van den Broek, 1994). What differentiates comprehension of a *text* from comprehension of a list of *sentences* is the detection
of meaningful relations between the sentences. If all goes well, the result
resembles a coherent network of nodes (the informational units from the text
and relevant background knowledge) and connections (the semantic relations
between the pieces of information).

A considerable amount of evidence supports the psychological validity of network representations (e.g., Graesser, 2007; Kintsch, 1998; van den Broek & Trabasso, 1986; van den Broek, Virtue, Everson, Tzeng & Sung, 2002; for reviews, see Singer, 1994, van den Broek, 1994). For instance, the likelihood of readers remembering individual pieces of information from a text is a linear function of the number of relations that each piece has to other information in the representation (e.g., Graesser & Clark, 1985; Trabasso & van den Broek, 1985). Reminding a reader of one part of the text speeds up recognition of parts that are connected in the network but distant in surface structure, more so than other parts that are unconnected but closer in surface structure (van den Broek & Lorch, 1993). These and other findings show that proficient readers are sensitive to the relational structure of a text, as captured by a network.

To construct a successful, coherent network, a reader infers relations among the text elements and, where necessary, to background knowledge he or she has accessed (van den Broek, 2010). To understand how readers do this—and to understand possible sources of differences among individual readers and potential causes for the construction of incomplete or incorrect representations—it helps to take a closer look at the inferential processes as they occur during reading.

Relations are most likely to be identified when the pieces of information that are to be related are activated simultaneously in working memory. As a reader progresses through a text, the concepts of working memory constantly change. A primary source of activated information in working memory consists, of course, of the idea units in the sentence currently being read. But other sources contribute to the contents of working memory as well. In particular, information from preceding text and from the reader's prior knowledge may be activated (see Table 3.1; van den Broek, 1990). Information from these sources may be activated through a combination of automatic and strategic processes, over cycles of processing.

Table 3.1. Creating coherence during reading: Mechanisms and sources of activation

1. Processing the current sentence	
2. Automatic processes	a. Carry over from preceding reading cycle
	b. Spread-of-activation or resonance to:
	— prior text
	— background knowledge
3. Strategic, coherence-building processes	a. Search of (memory for) prior text
	b. Recruitment of background knowledge
	c. Retrieval from other sources (e.g. other texts)

automatic - bottom up

With respect to the automatic processes, the two main mechanisms are carryover from the preceding processing cycle, whereby a subset of the information in working memory during one cycle will be retained into the next cycle (e.g., Kintsch & van Dijk, 1978), and spread of activation, or resonance, whereby concepts and events in the current cycle will automatically activate associated concepts and events from the reader's memory for preceding text and from his or her prior knowledge (Myers & O'Brien, 1998; O'Brien, 1995; O'Brien & Myers, 1999).

Skilled readers also have a large toolbox of strategic processes from which they can recruit to build coherence. One set of strategies involves retrieving or reinstating information from the preceding text. Information from the preceding text can be retrieved by rereading earlier parts of the text (e.g., Goldman & Saul, 1990) or by searching one's memory for these earlier parts. A second set of strategies involves activating information from prior knowledge by searching one's long-term semantic memory. Additional strategies include accessing other sources of information, such as looking for additional texts, searching the World Wide Web, and so on.

In all these cases, actual activation occurs through reading or otherwise processing the additional information. These strategies are *learned*, implicitly or explicitly, and with practice become increasingly automated (Laberge & Samuels, 1974; Thurlow & van den Broek, 1997). Over the course of reading a text, the combination of automatic and strategic processes result in a *landscape of activations* (Linderholm, Virtue, van den Broek & Tzeng, 2004; van den Broek, 2010; van den Broek, Rapp, & Kendeou, 2005; van den Broek, Young, Tzeng, & Linderholm, 1998), in which concepts fluctuate in their activation from sentence to sentence.

The extent to which the automatic processes are supplemented by strategic processes in a particular reading situation depends on the *standards of coherence* that a reader employs while reading a particular text. The standards of coherence reflect the extent of comprehension and coherence that the reader attempts to maintain (van den Broek, Bohn-Gettler, Kendeou, Carlson, & White, 2011; van den Broek et al., 1995; van den Broek, Lorch, Linderholm, & Gustafson, 2001); they determine both the types of relations that are identified and the strengths of those relations.

The standards vary across readers, for example as a function of metacomprehensive knowledge and skills (e.g., Schraw & Bruning, 1999); they can also vary across different reading situations for the same reader, for example as a function of motivation, the goal for reading a particular text, and so on (van den Broek, Lorch et al., 2001; van den Broek, Bohn-Gettler et al., 2012). If the activations from the automatic processes result in a degree of comprehension that meets the reader's standards, then no further strategic processes are needed and the reader continues to the next sentence. But if the degree of comprehension that the automatic processes allow does *not* meet the reader's standards of coherence, then strategic processes are likely to be recruited by the reader (van den Broek, Bohn-Gettler et al., 2012).

An important constraint on the strategic comprehension processes is that we have limited attentional capacity or working memory available to process information (first described in detail by Miller, 1956; see also Just & Carpenter, 1992). As a result, at any point during reading we can only process, or attend to, a subset of all potentially relevant pieces of information. Moreover, this limited capacity is used not only by comprehension processes but also other linguistic processes such as letter identification, decoding and other word processes, deciphering of grammatical structures, and so on.

The more attention that is claimed by these "lower level" processes, the less that is available for those at the level of the text as a whole (e.g., Perfetti et al., 2008; Jenkins, Fuchs, van den Broek, Espin & Deno, 2003a; 2003b). Conversely, the less capacity the lower-level processes demand (for instance, because of proficiency at these levels), the more attentional capacity that can be devoted to comprehension (Laberge & Samuels, 1974). Similarly, as some comprehension processes become automatized with practice, the reader can divert the freed-up resources to execute other, more complicated comprehension processes such as identifying themes, inferring abstract ideas, and so on (e.g., Thurlow & van den Broek, 1997).

In summary, central to the comprehension of a text is the construction of a coherent memory representation, by inferring relations between elements in the text, and between those elements and relevant background knowledge. This requires a balancing act, reconciling the limitations of attentional capacity and working memory with the standards of coherence that a reader wants.

In addition to automatic processes, readers use various strategic processes to allocate the precious remaining attentional resources. If successful, the reader will be able to identify relations between pieces of information that contribute to a coherent mental representation of the text; if attention is exhausted or improperly allocated (for example, in activating irrelevant information), then the mental representation will be suboptimal and comprehension will suffer.

INDIVIDUAL DIFFERENCES IN COMPREHENSION ABILITY

The above account of the reading process and product provides a framework for understanding individual and developmental differences in reading comprehension ability and, thereby, for conceptualizing tools for assessing comprehension. Variations among readers in component processes may lead to individual differences in reading comprehension ability.

Working Memory Capacity

Extensive research has shown that differences in attentional or working-memory capacity affect readers' ability to make inferences and create a coherent interpretation of a text. For example, readers with relatively small working memory capacity score lower on offline reading comprehension measures (including recall and question answering) than peers with higher capacity (e.g., Cain & Oakhill, 2007; Daneman & Carpenter, 1980; Linderholm & van den Broek, 2002). Low-capacity readers also are less likely to engage in the generation of inferences that contribute to a deeper understanding of a text.

For instance, compared to readers with high capacity, they tend to make fewer inferences that draw on background knowledge (Whitney, Ritchie, & Clark, 1991) or that anticipate/predict information that will come next in the text (Linderholm, 2002; Linderholm & van den Broek, 2002). They even create fewer basic, connecting inferences, in which currently read information is connected to preceding text ideas (e.g., Singer, Andrusiak, Reisdorf & Black, 1992; Trabasso & Magliano, 1996).

Background Knowledge

Background knowledge plays a crucial role in the establishment of coherence, as it allows readers to identify the often implicit semantic connections between text elements and to fill in inferential "blanks" in the text. A reader's background knowledge is activated by automatic processes but can also be accessed via strategic searches (Kintsch, 1988; van den Broek, 1990). If a reader lacks general background knowledge, or background knowledge on topics specific to a particular text, then comprehension and memory of the text will suffer (e.g., McNamara, Kintsch, Songer, & Kintsch, 1996).

Background knowledge can also extend to knowledge about texts and text structures in general. Such knowledge is useful in directing attention and inference generation to those aspects of a text that are likely to become relevant to the overall meaning of the text. Lack of such knowledge puts a reader at risk of failure to comprehend (Cain & Oakhill, 2007; Lynch et al., 2008; Williams, 1993).

Standards of Coherence

Readers' standards of coherence reflect the type and depth of coherence that they strive for in reading a particular text. These standards vary as a function of properties of the text and the reader's goal for reading a particular text (van den Broek, Bohn-Gettler et al., 2012), but there also may be consistent differences among individuals. For example, weak comprehenders adapt their standards less effectively to differing goals than do proficient readers (e.g., Cain & Oakhill, 2007; Linderholm & van den Broek, 2002). Such findings indicate that individuals differ not only in the strictness of their standards but also in their knowledge about different types of coherence (e.g., causal, temporal, spatial) and about the appropriateness of different standards for different reading situations.

Coherence-Building Strategies

When the automatic processes during reading do not allow readers to establish sufficient coherence to meet their standards, they can engage in strategic processes to strengthen the degree of comprehension (see, for instance, Table 3.1). Individuals differ in the range of strategies they possess as well as the efficiency with which they can execute them. For example, explanatory relations often span considerable distances in a text or may depend on the integration of multiple pieces of information. Identification of such relations requires not only that the reader recognizes a lack of coherence and accurately recruits the proper strategies (e.g., reinstatement or memory search for antecedents) but also that he or she can execute them properly and completely.

This example also illustrates that different components interact: Here the reader's working-memory capacity constraints influence the efficiency of strategy use. Altogether, differences in availability and efficiency of strategies result in different degrees of success in establishing coherence and understanding (e.g., Pressley & Hilden, 2005; Williams, 1993).

VOCABULARY

In the context of reading comprehension, background knowledge and vocabulary are closely related. The depth and breadth of a reader's vocabulary is the concrete, linguistic expression of his or her knowledge and, therefore, is the connecting point of text and the reader's knowledge. Individuals with better developed vocabularies tend to score better on many language tasks, including comprehension (e.g., Verhoeven & Perfetti, 2011). In longitudinal studies of language comprehension development, vocabulary at one age has been found to be among a limited set of strong predictors of comprehension at a later age (Kendeou, van den Broek, White & Lynch, 2009; van den Broek, Kendeou, et al., 2005).

These and other individual differences in component aspects of the comprehension process individually and in interaction lead to differences in the ability to create coherent representations of text and, hence, to comprehension differences. It is worth noting that even weak readers attempt to identify relations and construct representation (e.g., Cain & Oakhill, 2007; Linderholm et al., 2000).

Indeed, even children with (mild) Down Syndrome remember information with more semantic relations better than information with few relations (Kim, Kendeou, van den Broek, White & Kremer, 2008). Likewise, children with Attention Deficit and Hyperactivity Disorder (ADHD) are able to detect causal and other semantic relations, provided that their attention is not diverted by distractors (e.g., Lorch et al., 2004). Thus, variation in the component processes is likely to lead to differences in *degree* of coherence building and comprehension, rather than to categorical differences in terms of whether coherence is built.

A second important consideration is that there may be *subgroups* of weak readers, each with a unique *pattern* of processing. Those who have been identified as having reading comprehension problems tend to have patterns of processing that are clearly different from those of their well-reading peers. For example, fourth, seventh and ninth grade students who were identified as having reading comprehension difficulty by their teachers and through a battery of standardized tests showed distinct patterns of text processing as revealed by eye movements and think-aloud responses (Rapp, van den Broek, McMaster, Kendeou & Espin, 2007).

Interestingly, cluster analyses revealed that there were two distinct subgroups of struggling readers, both different in their processing from same-age good readers. One of these subgroups appeared to engage in very little inference generation beyond the sentence; the other appeared to engage in relation-building but with the relations involving relatively irrelevant pieces of information. Importantly, these subgroups were indistinguishable when compared on their standardized text scores or on their basis language skills. They only were identified by directly considering the inferential and attention allocation processes.

It is worth noting that some of the observed individual differences parallel the developmental patterns described below, but others are different. Through a clever design (Comprehension Age Matched, or CAM) in which they compared processing by good and weak comprehending children at one age to that by younger children who were matched in comprehension to the weak, older children, Cain and Oakhill (2007), were able to disentangle development from weakness. In a series of studies, these researchers showed that difficulties in comprehension ability do not simply reflect delays but represent a specific language impairment (SLI).

In summary, individual differences in the ability to relate different pieces of information in the text and background knowledge are associated with variations in reading comprehension. As comprehension is the outcome of a range of processes and cognitive factors, the causes for individual variation and reading comprehension difficulties can find their origin in different component processes and skill. To identify the unique pattern of processes and skills that brings about comprehension (or lack of comprehension) for a particular individual, diagnostic tools should be aimed at capturing an individual's standing on each of these components.

DEVELOPMENTAL DIFFERENCES IN COMPREHENSION

There has been extensive investigation of the development of comprehension skills in children. The findings of this research allow one to trace the development of many of the components of reading comprehension. A complete review of skills and processes is beyond the scope of this chapter, but several main points can be stated (for more complete reviews, see, for example, the volumes edited by van den Broek, Bauer & Bourg, 1997; Oakhill & Cain, 2007).

First, the nature of the memory representation that supports comprehension for young and beginning readers is similar to that of adults. For example, network representation also captures how young and beginning readers comprehend the texts they read. Beginning elementary school children demonstrate sensitivity to structural features of a text by systematically recalling events with many relations more often than events with few relations (Oakhill & Cain, 2007; Stein & Glenn, 1979; van den Broek & Kremer, 1999).

Similar patterns of ever-increasing sensitivity to semantic structure have been observed with other tasks, such as question answering, summarizing, theme identification, and so on (van den Broek et al., 2003; van den Broek, Tzeng, Risden, Trabasso & Basche, 2001; Williams, 1993). Indeed, investigation of preschool children's comprehension of narratives using media other than text (e.g., orally presented or televised) shows that children as young as four years old understand narratives by identifying relations between what they hear or see, and selectively recall events and facts with many connections (van den Broek, Kendeou, & White, 2009; van den Broek, Lorch & Thurlow, 1996).

When we consider comprehension and memory of concretely experienced simple event sequences such as building objects with blocks, even toddlers already appear to organize their world according to simple relations (Bauer, 1997). Thus, from a very young age onward, humans interpret and organize information that they encounter by identifying meaningful relations and constructing a coherent mental representation.

Second, although even very young children attempt to build coherent mental representations, their skills to do so are still developing. As a result, they identify relations and construct representations differently and less effectively than do older children and adults. This is evident, for example, in findings that the *degree to which* younger children selectively remember events with many connections is smaller than that for older children (e.g., van den Broek et al., 1996), and, in doing so, they tend to focus on different types of relations.

There may be structural reasons for such differences (for instance because their processing is less efficient, their use of working memory is still developing, and so on). There may also be experiential reasons (for instance, incomplete development of strategies for obtaining explanations from prior text and/or background knowledge, underdeveloped knowledge about standards of coherence, gaps in relevant background knowledge, and so on). As a consequence, there are systematic developmental differences in the kinds of relations that are efficiently detected.

These developmental differences can be categorized along several dimensions (van den Broek, 1997). One dimension concerns abstractness of relations. In general, young children most easily identify relations between overt, concrete events and ideas, whereas older children increasingly become capable of identifying relations between abstract or internal ideas, such as the goals or feelings of protagonists.

A second dimension concerns the scope of relations. Whereas younger children tend to focus on relations between individual events or facts, older children increasingly focus on relations involving clusters of events and ideas, allowing for the identification of themes or morals (e.g., Williams, 1993). Thus, there are systematic developmental differences in the ability to identify different types of meaningful relations and, hence, the richness and depth of the resulting mental representation of a text.

Third, individual differences in comprehension ability are remarkably stable across development. Indeed, results from longitudinal studies show that very young children's ability to comprehend narratives that they hear or see on television predicts their comprehension ability during reading several years later (Kendeou et al., 2009).

Interestingly, structural equation modeling shows that comprehension skills and basic language ("code-related") skills such as phonological awareness and decoding appear to form clusters of skills that develop relatively independently from each other (Kendeou et al., 2009; van den Broek, White, Kendeou & Carlson, 2009; see also Hoover & Gough, 1990, and Whitehurst

& Lonigan, 1998). When the child begins to read for comprehension, these two clusters come together, with each cluster contributing uniquely to variations in reading comprehension performance.

In summary, throughout life, comprehension revolves around the identification of relations between pieces of information and the gradual constructions of a coherent mental representation of that information. The skills to do so start developing at a very early age and have stability across development. When the child starts to read, the comprehension skills combine with language-specific skills such as word decoding to jointly predict reading comprehension performance.

THE ASSESSMENT OF READING COMPREHENSION ABILITY

The above conceptual framework of inference making and coherence construction during reading has implications for designing assessment tools. Individual variations in the component aspects of the comprehension process influence which relations a reader can detect in a text and, consequently, which relations are incorporated in the reader's mental representation at the completion of reading it. Several general observations and specific implications and recommendations follow.

Assessing for Different Purposes

When translating aspects of the comprehension process into assessment tools, it is important to be aware, as mentioned at the outset of this chapter, that the purpose for assessment of reading comprehension—and the accompanying practical constraints—will shape the tool to a considerable degree. For instance, if the purpose is to monitor the progress of students in an instructional program, the test needs to be short and easy to administer, and it should have multiple parallel versions to allow repeated administration.

For such a purpose, a lengthy comprehension test with multiple components would not be feasible. A more logical choice would be to design a simple test whose scores *correlate* with assessments of important aspects of comprehension, for example, tests developed under Curriculum-based Measurement (CBM; Deno & Fuchs, 1987; Espin, De La Paz, Scierka, & Roelofs, 2005; van den Broek & White, 2012). In contrast, if the purpose is to attain an in-depth assessment of an individual's skills and of possible causes for reading comprehension difficulties—for instance, for diagnosis or intervention—consideration of the processes and factors described in the preceding sections is likely to prove fruitful.

Conversely, the particular tasks and items that are included in an assessment tool influence how one views proficiencies of individual readers. For example, recent reviews of standardized reading comprehension tasks indicate that scores on these tests depend to a considerable degree on an individual's basic language skills such as phonological awareness, decoding, and so on, rather than comprehension skills per se.

Moreover, the tests differ in the particular combinations of basic skills that determine the scores and, hence, in their estimates of the comprehension skills of the individual (e.g., Keenan, Betjemann, & Olson, 2008; Nation & Snowling, 1997; Pearson & Hamm, 2005; Pressley & Hilden, 2005). In general, because reading comprehension is multifaceted and because each test samples a subset of these facets by its selection of tasks and item types, different tests capture different slices of comprehension as a whole.

Process and Product

Throughout the chapter, it has been emphasized that comprehension of a text involves the product that the reader has at the end of reading as well as the process by which the reader constructs this product. The process is where success or failure is achieved (cf. Pearson & Hamm, 2005). For some purposes (e.g., test of overall achievement), the assessment of the final product of comprehension is sufficient; measures of the representation, such as sensitivity to relational structure in recall for the text, would do the job in this case. For other purposes (e.g., to identify sources of strength and weakness and/ or to determine the most appropriate intervention for an individual), gaining insight into the processes by which an individual reader approaches the task of comprehending a text is required.

Construction of a Coherent Mental Representation

Central to successful reading comprehension is the construction of a coherent mental representation. This representation evolves from the automatic and strategic inferential processes in which the reader engages as he or she progresses through the text. The skills, strategies, and cognitive structures by which the reader identified meaningful relations between different parts of the text and between text and background knowledge are at the heart of comprehension.

Thus, comprehension is a multidimensional construct, a family of activities rather than a single process or outcome that one does or does not achieve. Two individuals may both "comprehend" a text but do so in different ways: for example, one may be able to give a detailed account of the sequence of events and facts, whereas the other may be able to state in a few words the precise gist. Moreover, strength in one component may to some extent compensate for weakness in another. For example, superb background knowledge about the topic of a text may mask weakness in inferential skills, and vice versa.

Developing an Assessment Tool

Assessment of reading comprehension should be aimed at determining an individual's skills, strategies, and cognitive structures in constructing a coherent representation—such as those described in the preceding sections on comprehension and individual /developmental differences. Such an assessment would resemble a scouting report by a sports coach, in which a (basketball) player obtains scores for shooting, rebounding missed shots, dribbling, and passing. Although it is possible to calculate a single score, representing the player's overall basketball prowess, the emphasis is on the fact that a player has a differentiated profile of skills and abilities.

To develop a reading comprehension assessment, several options exist. One option is to select the one or two components of comprehension that are central to the purpose for the assessment tool and ignore the others. For example, if the purpose is to assess one's ability to apply information from texts, then a test should measure that skill (or its component skills) instead of, for example, the skills involved in remembering or answering questions about the text.

A second option is to employ a suite of assessment tools, allowing one to describe the particular mix of skills for each individual (see also Magliano, Millis, Ozuru, & McNamara, 2007). By using different methods, one obtains a differentiated view of the profile of skills and abilities of individual readers. For example, one can use a combination of recall and summarization tasks to assess the outcome of comprehension or a combination of eye-tracking and think-aloud tasks to assess processing (e.g., Rapp et al, 2007).

A third option is to develop a single assessment tool that allows the identification of the various skills and abilities involved in comprehension. Although developing such a tool may be daunting, the combination of test-construction methods such as Item Response Theory (IRT) (e.g., De Boeck & Wilson, 2004) and detailed theories of reading comprehension hold considerable promise. The theoretical accounts allow the identification of locations in the text where specific processes (e.g., reinstatement from prior text, recruitment of relevant background knowledge) are to be executed by the reader. Using methods such as IRT, it may be possible to construct a limited set of texts and items that would allow evaluation of the major component processes.

Assessment could be done online, but it may be possible to construct off-line testing measures that are sensitive to differences seen in online processing. For example, using a clever design of materials, Kintsch and colleagues were able to use an offline verification task to determine the types of online processing in which their research participants had engaged (Kintsch, Welsch, Schmalhofer, & Zimny, 1990).

As noted above, successful reading comprehension often involves the identification of relations that span considerable distances in a text or the integration of multiple pieces of information. By using fairly lengthy texts that can be understood at different levels of complexity, one can construct offline test items that depend on the ability to detect relations across distance or among multiple text elements.

CONCLUDING REMARKS

The ability to comprehend texts is crucial for successful participation in society. It also is a complex cognitive task that is uniquely human. For both reasons it is important to gain insights in how readers accomplish the task, to determine what might go wrong in the process, and to decide on, and assess, the effectiveness of courses of action that address the core of an individual's problem. Over the course of reading, an individual engages in a complex "dance" of automatic and strategic processes by which one's limited attention is allocated to information from different sources—the current sentence, preceding text and background knowledge.

Out of these processes emerges a representation—a gradually evolving mental image of what the text is about. Understanding the choreography of this dance is not only fascinating, but also provides a powerful basis for constructing diagnostic tools and powerful interventions.

REFERENCES

Bauer, P. J. (1997). Development of memory in early childhood. In N. Cowan (Ed.), *The development of memory in childhood* (pp. 83–111). Sussex, U.K.: Psychology Press.

Baumann, J. (1983). Children's ability to comprehend main ideas in content textbooks. *Reading World, 22,* 322–31.

Cain, K. & Oakhill, J. (2007). Reading comprehension difficulties: Correlates, causes, and consequences. In K. Cain & J. Oakhill (Eds.), *Children's comprehension problems in oral and written language: A cognitive perspective* (pp. 41–75). New York: Guilford.

Cain, K., Oakhill, J., & Lemmon, K. (2004). Individual differences in the inference of word meanings from context: The influence of reading comprehension, vocabulary knowledge, and memory capacity. *Journal of Educational Psychology, 96,* 671–81.

Daneman, M., & Carpenter, P. A. (1980). Individual differences in working memory and reading. *Journal of Verbal Learning and Verbal Behavior, 19,* 450–66.

De Boeck, P., & Wilson, M. (Eds.) (2004). *Explanatory item response models. A generalized linear and nonlinear approach.* New York: Springer.

Deno, S. L., & Fuchs, L. S. (1987). Developing curriculum-based measurement systems for data-based special education problem solving. *Focus on Exceptional Children, 19,* 1–16.

Ehrlich, M. F. (1996). Metacognitive monitoring in the processing of anaphoric devices in skilled and less skilled comprehenders. In C. Cornoldi & J. V. Oakhill (Eds.), *Reading comprehension difficulties: Processes and remediation* (pp. 221–49). Mahwah, NJ: Lawrence Erlbaum Associates.

Espin, C. A., De La Paz, S., Scierka, B. J., & Roelofs, L. (2005). Relation between curriculum-based measures in written expression and quality and completeness of expository writing for middle-school students. *Journal of Special Education, 38,* 208–17.

Goldman, S. R., & Saul, E. U. (1990). Flexibility in text processing: A strategy competition model. *Learning and Individual Differences, 2,* 181–219.

Graesser, A. C. (2007). An introduction to strategic reading comprehension. In D. McNamara (Ed.), *Reading comprehension strategies: Theories, interventions, and technologies* (pp. 3–26). Mahwah, NJ: Lawrence Erlbaum Associates.

Graesser, A. C. & Clark, L. F. (1985). *Structures and procedures of implicit knowledge.* Norwood, NJ: Ablex.

Graesser, A. C., Singer, M., & Trabasso, T. (1994). Constructing inferences during narrative text comprehension. *Psychological Review, 101,* 371–95.

Greenberg, D., Ehri, L. C., & Perin, D. (1997). Are word-reading processes the same or different in adult literacy students and third-fifth graders matched for reading level? *Journal of Educational Psychology, 89,* 262–75.

Hoover, W., & Gough, P. B. (1990). The simple view of reading. *Reading and Writing, 2,* 127–60.

Jenkins, J. R., Fuchs, L.S., van den Broek, P., Espin, C., & Deno, S.L. (2003a). Sources of individual differences in reading comprehension and reading fluency. *Journal of Educational Psychology, 95,* 719–29.

Jenkins, J. R., Fuchs, L. S., van den Broek, P., Espin, C., & Deno, S. L. (2003b). Accuracy and fluency in list and context reading of skilled and RD groups: Absolute performance levels and sensitivity to impairment. *Learning Disabilities Research & Practice, 18,* 237–45.

Just, M. A., & Carpenter, P. A. (1992). A capacity theory of comprehension: Individual differences in working memory. *Psychological Review, 99,* 122–49.

Keenan, J. M. Betjemann, R. S. & Olson, R. K. (2008). Reading comprehension tests vary in the skills they assess: Differential dependence on decoding and oral comprehension. *Scientific Studies of Reading, 12,* 281–300.

Kendeou, P., van den Broek, P., White, M. J., & Lynch, J. (2009). Predicting reading comprehension in early elementary school: The independent contributions of oral language and code-related skills. *Journal of Educational Psychology, 4,* 765–78.

Kim, O., Kendeou, P, van den Broek, P., White, M. J., & Kremer, K. (2008). Cat, rat, and Rugrats: Narrative comprehension in young children with Down Syndrome. *Journal of Developmental and Physical Disabilities, 20,* 337–51.

Kintsch, W. (1988). The role of knowledge in discourse comprehension: A construction-integration model. *Psychological Review, 95,* 163–82.

———. (1998). *Comprehension: A paradigm for cognition.* New York: Cambridge University Press.

Kintsch, W. & van Dijk, T.A. (1978). Toward a model of text comprehension and production. *Psychological Review, 85,* 363–94.

Kintsch, W., Welsch, D., Schmalhofer, F., & Zimny, S. (1990). Sentence memory: A theoretical analysis. *Journal of Memory and Language, 29,* 133–59.

Laberge, D. & Samuels, S.J. (1974). Toward a theory of automatic information processing in reading. *Cognitive Psychology, 6,* 293–323.

Linderholm, T. (2002). Predictive inference generation as a function of working memory capacity and causal text constraints. *Discourse Processes, 34,* 259–80.

Linderholm, T., Gaddy, M., van den Broek, P., Mischinski, M., Crittenden, A., & Samuels, J. (2000). Effects of causal text revisions on more- and less-skilled readers' comprehension of easy and difficult texts. *Cognition and Instruction, 18,* 525–56.

Linderholm, T., & van den Broek, P. (2002). The effects of reading purpose and working memory capacity on the processing of expository text. *Journal of Educational Psychology,* 94, 778–84.

Linderholm, T., Virtue, S., van den Broek, P., & Tzeng, Y. (2004). Fluctuations in the availability of information during reading: Capturing cognitive processes using the landscape model. *Discourse Processes, 37,* 165–86.

Lorch, E. P., Eastham, D., Milich, R., Lemberger, C. L., Sanchez, R. P., Welsh, R., & van den Broek, P. (2004). Difficulties in comprehending causal relations among children with ADHD: The role of cognitive engagement. *Journal of Abnormal Psychology, 113,* 56–63.

Lynch, J. S., van den Broek, P., Kremer, K. E., Kendeou, P., White, M. J., & Lorch, E. P. (2008). The development of narrative comprehension and its relation to other early reading skills. *Reading Psychology, 29,* 327–65.

Magliano, J. P., Millis, K., Ozuru, Y., & McNamara, D. S. (2007). A multidimensional framework to evaluate assessment tools. In D.S. McNamara (Ed.), *Reading comprehension strategies: Theory, interventions, and technologies* (pp. 107–36). Mahwah, NJ: Lawrence Erlbaum Associates.

McNamara, D. S., Kintsch, E., Songer, N. & Kintsch, W. (1996). Are good texts always better? Interaction of text coherence, background knowledge, and levels of understanding. *Cognition & Instruction, 14,* 1–43.

Miller, G. A. (1956). The magical number seven, plus or minus two: Some limits on our capacity for processing information. *Psychological Review 63,* 81–97.

Myers, J. L & O'Brien, E. J. (1998). Accessing the discourse representation during reading. *Discourse Processes, 26,* 131–57.

Nation, K., & Snowling, M. (1997). Assessing reading difficulties: The validity and utility of current measures of reading skills. *British Journal of Educational Psychology, 67,* 359–70.

National Center for Education Statistics (2007). The nation's report card. Washington, D.C.: U.S. Department of Education, Institution of Education Sciences, National Center for Educational Statistics. Retrieved June 15, 2008 from http://nces.ed.gov/nationsreportcard/.

Oakhill, J. & Cain, K. (2007). Introduction to comprehension development. In K. Cain & J. Oakhill (Eds.), *Children's comprehension problems in oral and written language: A cognitive perspective* (pp. 41–75). New York: Guilford Press.

O'Brien, E. (1995). Automatic components of discourse comprehension. In R. F. Lorch, Jr. & E. O'Brien (Eds.), *Sources of coherence in reading* (pp. 159–76). Hillsdale, NJ: Lawrence Erlbaum Associates.

O'Brien, E. J., & Myers, J. L. (1999). Text comprehension: A view from the bottom up. In S. R. Goldman, A. C. Graesser, & P. van den Broek (Eds.), *Narrative comprehension, causality, and coherence* (pp. 35-53). Mahwah, NJ: Lawrence Erlbaum Associates.

Paris, S. G., Carpenter, R. D., Paris, A. H., & Hamilton, E. E. (2005). Spurious and genuine correlates of children's reading comprehension. In S. G. Paris & S. A. Stahl (Eds.), *Children's reading comprehension and assessment* (pp. 131–60). Mahwah, NJ: Lawrence Erlbaum Associates.

Pearson, P. D., & Hamm, D. N. (2005). The assessment of reading comprehension: A review of practices—past, present, and future. In S. G. Paris & S. A. Stahl (Eds.), *Children's reading comprehension and assessment* (pp. 13–69). Mahwah, NJ: Lawrence Erlbaum Associates.

Perfetti, C., Yang, C-L. & Schmalhofer, F. (2008). Comprehension skill and word-to-text integration process. *Applied Cognitive Psychology, 22,* 303–18.

Perie, M., Grigg, W., and Donahue, P. (2005). *The nation's report card: Reading 2005* (NCES 2006–451). Washington, D.C.: U.S. Department of Education, Institute of Education Sciences, National Center for Education Statistics.

Pressley, M., & Hilden, K. R. (2005). Commentary on three important directions in comprehension assessment research. In S. Paris & S. Stahl (Eds.), *Children's reading comprehension and assessment* (pp. 305–18). Mahwah, NJ: Lawrence Erlbaum Associates.

Rapp, D. N., van den Broek, P., McMaster, K. L., Kendeou, P., & Espin, C. A. (2007). Higher-order comprehension processes in struggling readers: A perspective for research and intervention. *Scientific Studies of Reading, 11,* 289–312.

Schraw, G. & Bruning, R. (1999). How implicit models of reading affect motivation to read and reading engagement. *Scientific Studies of Reading, 3,* 281–302.

Singer, M. (1994). Discourse inference processes. In M. A. Gernsbacher (Ed.), *Handbook of psycholinguistics* (pp. 479–515). New York: Academic Press.

Singer, M., Andrusiak, P., Reisdorf, P., & Black, N. L. (1992). Individual differences in bridging inference processes. *Memory & Cognition, 20,* 539–48.

Stein, N. L., & Glenn, C. G. (1979). An analysis of story comprehension in elementary school children. In R. O. Freedle (Ed.), *New direction in discourse processing* (vol. 2, pp. 53–120). Hillsdale, NJ: Lawrence Erlbaum Associates.

Thurlow, R. & van den Broek, P. (1997). Automaticity in inference generation during reading. *Reading and Writing Quarterly, 13,* 165–81.

Trabasso, T., & Magliano, J. P. (1996). How do children understand what they read and what can we do to help them? In M. Graves, P. van den Broek, & B. Taylor (Eds.), *The first R: A right of all children* (pp. 160–88). New York: Columbia University Press.

Trabasso, T., Secco, T., & van den Broek, P. W. (1984). Causal cohesion and story coherence. In H. Mandl, N. L. Stein & T. Trabasso (Eds.), *Learning and comprehension of text* (pp. 83–111). Hillsdale, NJ: Lawrence Erlbaum Associates.

Trabasso, T., & van den Broek, P. W. (1985). Causal thinking and the representation of narrative events. *Journal of Memory and Language, 24,* 612–30.

van den Broek, P. W. (1990). Causal inferences in the comprehension of narrative texts. In A. C. Graesser and G. H. Bower (Eds.), *Psychology of learning and motivation: Inferences and text comprehension* (vol. 25, pp. 175–96). New York, NY: Academic Press.

———. (1994). Comprehension and memory of narrative texts: Inferences and coherence. In M. A. Gernsbacher (Ed.), *Handbook of psycholinguistics* (pp. 539–88). New York: Academic Press.

———. (1997). Discovering the cement of the universe: The development of event comprehension from childhood to adulthood. In P. van den Broek, P. Bauer, & T. Bourg (Eds.), *Developmental spans in event comprehension and representation: Bridging fictional and actual events* (pp. 321–42). Hillsdale, NJ: Lawrence Erlbaum Associates.

———. (2010). Using texts in science education: Cognitive processes and knowledge representation. *Science, 328,* 453–56.

van den Broek, P., Bauer, P., & Bourg, T. (Eds.) (1997). *Developmental spans in event comprehension and representation: Bridging fictional and actual events.* Hillsdale, NJ: Lawrence Erlbaum Associates.

van den Broek, P., Bohn-Gettler, C., Kendeou, P., Carlson, S., & White, M. J. (2011). When a reader meets a text: The role of standards of coherence in reading comprehension. In M. T. McCrudden, J. P. Magliano, & G. Schraw (Eds.), *Text relevance and learning from text.* (pp. 123–140). Greenwich, CT: Information Age Publishing.

van den Broek, P., Kendeou, P., Kremer, K., Lynch, J. S., Butler, J., White, M. J., & Lorch, E. P. (2005). Assessment of comprehension abilities in young children. In S. Paris & S. Stahl (Eds.), *Children's reading comprehension and assessment* (pp. 107–30). Mahwah, NJ: Lawrence Erlbaum Associates.

van den Broek, P., Kendeou, P., & White, M. J. (2009). Cognitive processes during reading: Implications for the use of multimedia to foster reading comprehension. In A. G. Bus & S. B. Neuman (Eds.), *Multimedia and literacy development: Improving achievement for young learners* (pp. 57–73). New York: Taylor & Francis.

van den Broek, P., & Kremer, K. (1999). The mind in action: What it means to comprehend. In B. Taylor, M. Graves, & P. van den Broek (Eds.), *Reading for meaning* (pp.1-31). New York: Teacher's College Press.

van den Broek, P.W., Lorch, E. P., & Thurlow, R. (1996). Children's and adults' memory for television stories: The role of causal factors, story-grammar categories and hierarchical level. *Child Development, 67,* 3010–29.

van den Broek, P. W., & Lorch, R. F. Jr. (1993). Network representations of causal relations in memory for narrative texts: Evidence from primed recognition. *Discourse Processes, 16,* 75–98.

van den Broek, P., Lorch, R. F. Jr, Linderholm, T., & Gustafson, M. (2001). The effects of readers' goals on inference generation and memory for texts. *Memory & Cognition, 29,* 1081–87.

van den Broek, P., Lynch, J. S., Naslund, J., Ievers-Landis, C. E., & Verduin, K. (2003). The development of comprehension of main ideas in narratives: Evidence from the selection of titles. *Journal of Educational Psychology 95,* 707–18.

van den Broek, P., Rapp, D. N., & Kendeou, P. (2005). Integrating memory-based and constructionist processes in accounts of reading comprehension. *Discourse Processes, 39,* 299–316.

van den Broek, P., Risden, K., & Husebye-Hartman, E. (1995). The role of readers' standards for coherence in the generation of inferences during reading. In R. F. Lorch, Jr. & E. J. O'Brien (Eds.), *Sources of coherence in text comprehension* (pp. 353–73). Hillsdale, NJ: Lawrence Erlbaum Associates.

van den Broek, P. W., & Trabasso, T. (1986). Causal networks versus goal-hierarchies in summarizing text. *Discourse Processes, 9,* 1–15.

van den Broek, P., Tzeng, Y., Risden, K., Trabasso, T., & Basche, P. (2001). Inferential questioning: Effects on comprehension of narrative texts as a function of grade and timing. *Journal of Educational Psychology, 93,* 521–29.

van den Broek, P., Virtue, S., Everson, M., Tzeng, Y., & Sung, Y. (2002). Comprehension and memory of science texts: Inferential processes and the construction of a mental representation. In J. Otero, J. Leon, & A. C. Graesser (Eds.), *The psychology of science text comprehension* (pp. 131–54). Mahwah, NJ: Lawrence Erlbaum Associates.

van den Broek, P. W. & White, M. J. (2012). Cognitive processes in reading and the measurement of comprehension. In C.A. Espin, K. McMaster & S. Rose (Eds.), *A measure of success: How CBM has influenced education and learning.* Minneapolis: University of Minnesota Press.

van den Broek, P., White. M. J., Kendeou, P., & Carlson, S. (2009). Reading between the lines: Developmental and individual differences in cognitive processes in reading comprehension. In R. Wagner, C. Schatschneider, & C. Phythian-Sence (Eds.), *Beyond decoding: The behavioral and biological foundations of reading comprehension* (pp. 107–23). New York: Guilford.

van den Broek, P., Young, M., Tzeng, Y., & Linderholm, T. (1998). The landscape model of reading: Inferences and the on-line construction of a memory representation. In H. van Oostendorp & S. R. Goldman (Eds.), *The construction of mental representations during reading* (pp. 71–98). Mahwah, NJ: Lawrence Erlbaum Associates.

Verhoeven, L., Biemond, H., Gijsel, M., & Netten, A. (2007). Taalvaardigheid Nederlands: Stand van zaken in 2007. (Reading proficiency in the Netherlands: The status in 2007). Nijmegen, The Netherlands: Expertisecentrum Nederlands.

Verhoeven, L., & Perfetti, C. A. (Eds.) (2011). Special issue: Vocabulary growth and reading skill. *Scientific Studies of Reading, 15,* 1–108.

Whitehurst, G. J. & Lonigan, C. J. (1998). Child development and emergent literacy. *Child Development, 69,* 848–72.

Whitney, P., Ritchie, B. G., & Clark, M. B. (1991). Working-memory capacity and the use of elaborative inferences in text comprehension. *Discourse Processes, 14,* 133–45.

Williams, J.P. (1993). Comprehension of students with and without learning disabilities: Identification of narrative themes and idiosyncratic text representations. *Journal of Educational Psychology, 85,* 631–42.

Williams, J. P. Stafford, K. B., Lauer, K. D., Hall, K. M., & Pollini, S. (2009). Embedding reading comprehension training in content-area instruction. *Journal of Educational Psychology, 101,* 1–20.

Chapter Four

Reading Comprehension Development from Seven to Fourteen Years: Implications for Assessment

Kate Cain & Jane Oakhill

We read to understand and to acquire information in a wide range of educational, academic, employment, and social situations, such as studying a history textbook in school, reading a journal article in preparation to write this chapter, following a recipe in a cookbook, catching up with friends on social networking sites, weighing the evidence in a newspaper article about climate change, or simply enjoying a novel at bedtime. From this perspective, an assessment of reading ability should be, in essence, a measure of reading comprehension: our ability to understand and remember what we read.

Reading comprehension is determined by a wide range of cognitive skills, knowledge, and processes. To understand the core of what we read, we need to decode the words, access their meanings, compute sentence meanings, and integrate information from different parts of the text and with our general knowledge, ultimately constructing an integrated and coherent representation of the meaning of the text. When viewed in this way, the development of a thorough and adequate assessment of reading comprehension looks to be a formidable task.

In this chapter, we review our work on reading comprehension development and difficulties and evaluate how this research can inform the assessment of reading comprehension.

SOURCES OF DISCOURSE COMPREHENSION FAILURE IN YOUNG READERS

The majority of children acquire adequate word reading and reading comprehension skills. Yet, a significant proportion of readers fail to do so. It is estimated that up to 10 percent of young readers are dyslexic: They encounter significant difficulty with word reading and spelling, with a phonological deficit at the core of their problems (Snowling, 2000).

Other young readers do not meet the classification of developmental dyslexia but experience both word reading and reading comprehension problems. These children are sometimes referred to as garden-variety poor readers (Gough & Tunmer, 1986). Their reading comprehension difficulties are considered secondary to their word reading problems, the result of slow or inefficient word processing skills (Perfetti, 1985).

However, an additional group of poor readers (up to 10 percent of children aged eight to eleven years) attain reading comprehension levels that are significantly below both their chronological age *and* word reading ability (Yuill & Oakhill, 1991). Their listening comprehension (assessed from their understanding of texts read aloud) is also impaired (Cain, Oakhill, & Bryant, 2000a); evidence that, for these children, word reading difficulties are not the source of their reading (and listening) comprehension problems.

In this group, the reading comprehension deficit can be eighteen months or greater (Cain & Oakhill, 2007) and, similar to children with dyslexia, poor comprehenders do not "grow out" of their reading difficulties without remediation (Cain & Oakhill, 2006). A sensitive and adequate assessment of reading comprehension must, therefore, tap more than an individual's word reading skills if it is to adequately discriminate these different groups of poor readers.

Literacy disorders, such as dyslexia and poor comprehension, are typically characterized by broad definitions. However, different research groups and clinicians use different selection criteria. For example, the selection criteria for dyslexics might include a full scale IQ score of 80 or above (Katzir, Young-Suk, Wolf, Morris, & Lovett, 2008) or verbal IQ of at least 90 (Altemeier, Abbott, & Berninger, 2008). Good and poor comprehenders are usually matched for word reading skills, but sometimes these are assessed by measures of word reading in context (Oakhill, 1982) or sometimes by nonword reading (Nation & Snowling, 1999). Readers should, therefore, bear in mind that the reported prevalence of these literacy disorders may differ because of definitional and sampling differences.

Characteristics of Poor Comprehenders

In our research, we have focused on comprehension of discourse, written or spoken text of more than a single sentence, in children and adolescents aged between seven and fourteen years selected for age-appropriate word reading. Poor comprehenders identified with this profile have good nonword reading and phonological processing skills (Cain, Oakhill, & Bryant, 2000b; Stothard

& Hulme, 1996) in contrast to children with developmental dyslexia. The levels of performance on these selection measures for typical groups of good and poor comprehenders are shown in Table 4.1. We refer the interested reader to Cain et al. (2000a) for a more detailed description of selection issues.

We have typically compared good and poor comprehenders matched for their level of written vocabulary knowledge: that is, the two groups are equally able to match pictures to printed words or provide synonyms for target words in short phrases. When chosen in this way, poor comprehenders also have good receptive vocabulary skills (Cain, Oakhill, & Lemmon, 2004).

However, the extent to which vocabulary skills are intact in this population has not been fully evaluated. The vocabulary tasks used to assess knowledge in our selection process have typically focused on breadth (number of words known) rather than depth (the richness and interconnectedness of the semantic network) (Ouellette, 2006). Indeed, some children with reading comprehension difficulties have semantic processing difficulties, which are evidenced in priming studies (Nation & Snowling, 1999).

Vocabulary knowledge and reading comprehension are highly correlated, and it is clear that if too many words are unknown, then reading for meaning is disrupted. In addition, a rich and interconnected semantic network may be necessary for fast and efficient text integration (Perfetti, 2007), a skill that is fundamental to discourse comprehension (and which is described in more detail below).

Table 4.1. Typical characteristics of good and poor comprehenders matched for word reading and reading vocabulary knowledge, and a younger comprehension-age match group

	Poor comprehenders	Good comprehenders	Comprehension-age match group
chronological age	8,0 (SD=4 mos)	8,0 (SD=4 mos)	7,0 (SD=3 mos)
reading vocabulary	41.3 (SD=2.06)	41.6 (SD=2.22)	34 (SD=3.46)
word reading accuracy in context	8,9 (SD=9 mos)	8,9 (SD=10 mos)	6,8 (SD=4 mos)
reading comprehension	6,9 (SD=4 mos)	9,3 (SD=13 mos)	6,10 (SD=4 mos)

Note. Where appropriate, ages are given as years, months. Maximum score for sight vocabulary test is 45.

Therefore, a certain level of vocabulary knowledge is necessary for reading to progress, but there is no evidence that knowledge of the relevant vocabulary is sufficient for good comprehension. Moreover, direct instruction in vocabulary has met with mixed success (for reviews, see Beck & McKeown, 1991; Mezynski, 1983), though most children and adults are adept at developing their vocabulary knowledge through reading (Stanovich, 1993).

An alternative way of looking at vocabulary development is not as a separable skill but more generally as a by-product of comprehension skills and strategies. We would argue that inference and metacognitive skills in particular are crucial in this respect: In much the same way that readers can extract new, or develop existing, knowledge from a text, they can also apply strategies to work out the meanings of unknown (or nuance the meanings of known) vocabulary items. From this perspective, comprehension skills are at least as important to vocabulary development as vocabulary knowledge is to comprehension.

The relation between reading comprehension and vocabulary is most likely reciprocal. Although much early vocabulary is taught through direct instruction and oral communication in the "here and now," vocabulary weaknesses may *emerge* during the course of development as children become independent readers. Written texts are a rich source of new vocabulary knowledge (Cunningham & Stanovich, 1998).

Acquisition of vocabulary through reading may be influenced by different factors. First, there is clear evidence that reading habits are related to vocabulary differences in older readers (Cain & Oakhill, 2011; Stanovich, 1986). Second, children with poor text comprehension skills have poor word learning and inference strategies (Cain, Oakhill, & Lemmon, 2004; Cain, Oakhill, & Elbro, 2003), which may restrict their ability to take advantage of vocabulary learning opportunities when reading. Thus, there is still much to understand about the relation between vocabulary and discourse comprehension during development.

Skill Weaknesses that Contribute to Discourse Comprehension Failure

Successful comprehension of written (or spoken) discourse results in an integrated and coherent representation of the meaning of a text (Kintsch, 1998). When we consider comprehension of discourse, we need to consider the skills and processes that enable a reader to construct a *situation model,* an integrated and coherent representation of the text's meaning.

It is clear that word recognition and reading fluency are linked with competence in reading comprehension (see, e.g., Catts, Hogan, & Fey, 2003;

Speece, Roth, Cooper, & De La Paz, 1999; Vellutino, Tunmer, Jaccard, & Chen, 2007). Likewise, vocabulary in the early school years has been found to be an important correlate of reading comprehension skill (e.g., Nation & Snowling, 2004; Vellutino et al., 2007). However, as we pointed out above, the link between vocabulary and comprehension is likely to be reciprocal, and the learning of new vocabulary is likely to depend on the skills and strategies that are important for other aspects of comprehension.

In our own investigations of the type of poor comprehender described above, we have identified a number of skills, in addition to word reading and vocabulary knowledge, that are important for successful discourse comprehension and which should be considered as potential causal factors in successful comprehension development. In this section, we review the importance of three skills that aid the construction of a coherent and integrated representation of meaning: inference and integration, comprehension monitoring, and knowledge and use of story structure.

Next, we provide examples of the tasks we have used to assess these abilities, and we consider the value of including such measures in assessments of reading comprehension skill. We do not wish to imply that these are the only skills that contribute to effective reading comprehension, but these have been demonstrated to have strong links to comprehension skill. Other aspects of reading comprehension skill, such as word reading and vocabulary, are important, of course, but these are typically assessed in any case when measuring reading ability. More detailed reviews can be found in Cain and Oakhill (2007).

Inference and Integration

Inference and integration are central to successful comprehension. Authors do not make every detail explicit in a text. As a consequence, readers must generate links between different parts of the text in order to integrate their meanings and use general knowledge to make inferences to fill in missing details. Although pre-readers are capable of making inferences (Kendeou, Bohn-Gettler, White, & van den Broek, 2008), inference and integration skills develop and improve substantially between the ages of six and fifteen years (Barnes, Dennis, & Haefele-Kalvaitis, 1996; Casteel, 1993).

A number of cross-sectional studies have demonstrated that good and poor comprehenders matched for chronological age and word reading differ in their ability on tasks that require the integration of sentences and inference generation (e.g., Bowyer-Crane & Snowling, 2005; Cain, Oakhill, Barnes, & Bryant, 2001; Oakhill, 1982, 1984).

Evidence that poor comprehenders are less likely to integrate information from different sentences in a text comes from an early study by Oakhill

(1982). In that study, good and poor comprehenders listened to short three-line texts. They subsequently completed a sentence recognition test in which they had to judge whether or not a test sentence had been presented in one of the short passages. Good comprehenders were more likely than poor comprehenders to falsely recognize new test sentences that combined information from two of the original sentences. This finding suggests that the good comprehenders had encoded an integrated memory representation of each text.

Further, in a study using the comprehension-age match design (Cain & Oakhill, 1999), we have found evidence that at least some aspects of inference skill may be causally implicated in comprehension development. In this study, poor comprehenders were significantly less likely to generate inferences by integrating information from different sentences in short narratives than younger readers at the same level of comprehension skill. These studies (and work with adults, e.g., Long & Chong, 2001; Millis & Graesser, 1994) strongly indicate that comprehension involves more than memory for the verbatim information in a text: Inference and integration are crucial for successful comprehension. An assessment of comprehension needs to measure these skills.

Comprehension Monitoring

Inferences and integration are needed to make a text cohere, but readers can only actively generate an inference if they are monitoring their understanding of the text. If the current sentence cannot be integrated with the situation model that a reader has constructed, he or she needs to take remedial action, which can involve generating an inference to establish a link. Comprehension monitoring thus appears to be important for successful comprehension. It can be detected in pre-readers (Skarakis-Doyle, 2002) but develops further during the years when reading fluency develops (Baker, 1984; Markman & Gorin, 1981).

A typical assessment of comprehension monitoring involves error detection. Children read (or listen) to short texts containing different types of error. The errors may involve an internal inconsistency, where information in one sentence contradicts an earlier statement in the text, or from an external inconsistency, where the information in the text conflicts with general knowledge. Other types of error can be created at the sentence level, by muddling the word order, or at the word level, through the use of nonsense words. To do well on these tasks, readers must actively engage in the evaluation of their understanding. In particular, inconsistencies are only detected if the reader seeks to integrate each successive sentence with the situation model of the text constructed so far, and with his or her general knowledge.

Children with poor reading comprehension have difficulties with comprehension monitoring, as measured by error detection tasks. For example, ten-year-old poor comprehenders are less likely to spot two contradictory sentences in a text (Oakhill, Hartt, & Samols, 2005), and ten- to fifteen-year-old French speakers are less likely to spot inconsistent anaphors (Ehrlich, 1996; Ehrlich, Remond, & Tardieu, 1999). These measures demonstrate the generality of poor comprehenders' difficulties, because they typically involve expository texts.

Poor comprehenders' difficulties in detecting internal inconsistencies are more pronounced when the two statements are separated by several filler lines of text. Furthermore, performance on these tasks is related to independent measures of working memory capacity (e.g., Oakhill, Hartt, & Samols, 2005). Thus, some of the problems that poor comprehenders experience with integration and comprehension monitoring may be due to weak memory skills.

Narrative: Knowledge and Use of Structure

Children are familiar with narratives from a very early age. Narrative text structure typically consists of a sequence of causally related events (Stein & Trabasso, 1982). An understanding of the structure of narratives develops early through being read stories by adults and making sense of events in everyday life (Mason, 1992; Trabasso & Stein, 1997). Comprehension and understanding of story structure is a foundation for later reading comprehension.

Knowledge and use of story structure can be assessed with production tasks. These do not involve word reading, and they enable the assessment of narrative structure and understanding in pre-readers and children with word reading difficulties (Paris & Paris, 2003). On such measures, seven- to eight-year-olds with poor reading comprehension are less likely to produce causally related sequences of events than same-age peers—their stories typically comprise a list of events—even when the storytelling task is supported by a series of pictures or a goal-directed title, such as "How the pirates lost their treasure" (Cain, 2003; Cain & Oakhill, 1996).

Similar deficits have been found for written story production (Cragg & Nation, 2006). Again we have evidence that poor knowledge and use of story structure is a potential source of comprehension failure: Poor comprehenders tell more poorly structured stories than a younger comprehension-age match group (Cain & Oakhill, 1996).

Poor comprehenders' difficulties with narrative extend beyond production tasks: Their ability to sequence short stories correctly when presented as individual sentences in an "anagram" task is poor (Cain & Oakhill, 2006).

Further, they appear to have difficulty identifying the essence of a story. They are poor at discriminating between the main point, the setting, and the main event of short stories (Yuill & Oakhill, 1991). Their difficulties do not extend to all elements of narrative; in contrast, their knowledge about the conventions used to begin and end stories is good (Cain, 1996).

Together, this body of work suggests that comprehension failure may arise because of difficulties with a wide range of language skills. Some children may experience reading comprehension difficulties because of poorly developed word reading or vocabulary skills; however, other children experience reading and listening comprehension problems despite adequate word reading and vocabulary skills. Similar groups have been identified in other countries and with other language groups (Catts, Adlof, & Weismer, 2006; Ehrlich & Remond, 1997; McGee & Johnson, 2003; Megherbi & Ehrlich, 2005; Nesi, Levorato, Roch, & Cacciari, 2006), suggesting that this profile is not simply a product of the British educational system.

This latter group of poor comprehenders show consistent problems with the skills that enable readers (and listeners) to extract meaning from text and construct coherent and integrated representations of a text's meaning. Thus, their problems with discourse comprehension appear to arise because of difficulties with the skills essential to reading for meaning.

READING COMPREHENSION DEVELOPMENT: LONGITUDINAL STUDIES

Our understanding of the factors that foster and facilitate reading comprehension development is less developed than our knowledge about word reading development. However, convergent with the research on poor comprehenders, longitudinal studies of reading development strongly suggest that skills in addition to word reading and vocabulary are crucial to the development of discourse comprehension skills.

One study, by de Jong and van der Leij (2002), looked at young readers between ages seven and ten. They found that vocabulary knowledge at age seven helped to explain a child's reading comprehension ability at age ten, after controlling for initial levels of word reading and, importantly, reading comprehension. Significantly, vocabulary knowledge did not account for variance in reading comprehension after controlling for the relationship between listening and reading comprehension. Although this study did not "unpack" the listening comprehension measure into the discourse-level skills discussed above, it strongly suggests that comprehension above the word level makes a unique contribution to a child's standard of reading comprehension.

Van den Broek and colleagues have investigated how pre-readers' language skills provide the foundation for later reading comprehension. Their work establishes an important link between narrative abilities across a range of media. Concurrent measures of comprehension of aural and audiovisual (televised) narratives in four- and six-year-old children are correlated, and comprehension of these media are additionally correlated with reading comprehension in eight-year-olds (Kendeou et al., 2008). Further, the ability to generate inferences when comprehending these narratives is related to a composite measure of general narrative comprehension. Finally, comprehension of aural and televised narratives at age six predicts reading comprehension at eight years above basic language skills (Kendeou, van den Broek, White, & Lynch, 2009).

This work with young readers and preschoolers suggests that early comprehension is more than simply word comprehension, i.e., vocabulary, or word reading. Further, there is evidence from a study by Kendeou et al. (2008) that the foundations of reading comprehension can be separated; in that study, inference and narrative comprehension were not wholly the same thing. In our own work, we have aimed to look at the importance of specific discourse processing skills—integration and inference, knowledge and use of story structure, and comprehension monitoring—to the development of reading comprehension in young readers.

These skills are all related to more general measures of reading comprehension and draw, to some extent, on the same pool of other skills and knowledge, such as vocabulary and memory (Cain, Oakhill, & Bryant, 2004). However, there is also evidence from the strength of their associations (Cain, Oakhill, & Bryant, 2004) and from profiles of skill strengths and weaknesses in poor comprehenders (Cain & Oakhill, 2006; Cornoldi, de Beni, & Pazzaglia, 1996) that these skills are, to some extent, separable.

Further, training studies have typically focused on just one of these skills, such as inference (McGee & Johnson, 2003; Yuill & Oakhill, 1988), story structure (Dimino, Gersten, Carnine, & Blake, 1990), and monitoring (Beal, Garrod, & Bonitatibus, 1990). For these reasons, it is important to determine whether these skills make independent contributions to reading comprehension development.

We next describe a longitudinal study in which we followed the progress of children from ages seven to eight until they turned ages thirteen to fourteen. There is a large body of evidence to show that specific phonological and literacy-related skills, such as letter knowledge, make unique contributions to the prediction of word reading in developing readers (Muter, Hulme, Snowling, & Stevenson, 2004).

The principal aim of our longitudinal study was to see if a similar pattern was true of reading comprehension; we sought to determine if the separate discourse-related skills we implicated in poor reading comprehension predict growth in comprehension of written text. In addition, we sought to identify whether early competence in these skills explained later reading comprehension skill, or whether the relative importance of these skills emerges late in reading comprehension development, as texts become more complex and rely to a greater extent on text processing skills.

To this end, we assessed a range of skills in young readers when they were aged seven to eight years, eight to nine years, and ten to eleven years, including reading comprehension (using a standardized measure of passage comprehension) and word reading accuracy; verbal and performance IQ; phonological awareness; receptive vocabulary; receptive syntax; working memory; and measures of three comprehension related skills—inference making, comprehension monitoring, and knowledge and use of story structure. Our sample comprised 101 children at the outset and was unselected: comprehension, vocabulary and other skills were free to vary. Here we present data for the 83 children (47 girls, 36 boys) for whom we have almost complete data from all three time points (three children missed one of the test sessions).

We derived path models to model the longitudinal relations between the observed variables in the prediction of Time 3 comprehension, using Amos 16 software. The final model, in which only remaining significant paths appear, is shown in Figure 4.1 with standardized coefficients. Full details of the analyses can be found in Oakhill and Cain (2012).

Initial reading comprehension skill was a strong predictor of later reading comprehension, and verbal ability (vocabulary and verbal IQ) also made significant contributions to the prediction of comprehension ability across time. Nevertheless, three distinct predictors of comprehension skill emerged, either through direct or indirect links: answering inferential questions, monitoring comprehension (by detecting inconsistencies in text), and knowledge and use of story structure (assessed by the ability to reconstruct a story from a set of jumbled sentences). These factors predicted comprehension at a later time even after the autoregressive effect of comprehension (the prediction of comprehension at later times from comprehension at earlier times) was controlled.

From these analyses, a picture of skill development emerges in which certain components of comprehension are predictive of general comprehension skill. Early abilities in inference skill, comprehension monitoring, and knowledge and use of story structure all predict a later global assessment of comprehension skill independent of the contribution of earlier comprehension skill, and over and above vocabulary and verbal IQ. In contrast, word reading accuracy was predicted by word-level skills: vocabulary and phonological awareness. Surprisingly, we did not find a direct relation between working

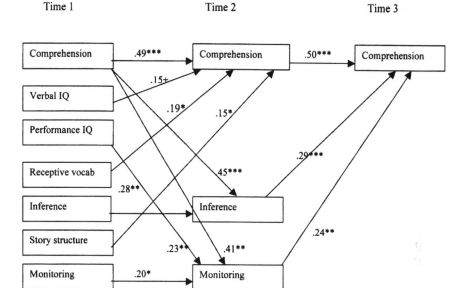

*** <.001, **.01, * .05, + .06

Figure 4.1. **Path diagram illustrating the relations between skills from Time One to Time Three reading comprehension.**

memory and reading comprehension. It is likely that the variance associated with working memory was shared by the discourse processing measures.

We were able to revisit fifty participants from this sample six years after the initial assessment, when the children were now aged thirteen to fourteen years. Here we used a different measure of reading comprehension, suitable for this age group, which includes subtests to assess skimming and inferential comprehension.

Early assessments of all three discourse-processing skills were found to be related to a composite of this later reading comprehension measure. It was not possible to extend the path analyses described earlier to include the later time point since the global comprehension assessments were not the same and the sample was much reduced in size. Instead, we conducted multiple regression analyses using the measures taken when our sample were aged ten to eleven years to predict later reading comprehension (and decoding skill) at ages thirteen to fourteen (Time 4).

First, we controlled for general verbal ability and earlier reading comprehension level by entering verbal IQ and reading comprehension measured when the children were aged ten to eleven years. We then entered all measures (word reading, vocabulary, syntax, memory, and the three discourse processing measures) taken at age ten to eleven years, using a forward step-wise procedure.

We found that after controlling for verbal IQ and comprehension at ten to eleven years, measures of story structure understanding, comprehension monitoring, inference skills and working memory each accounted for significant independent variance in the outcome measure: reading comprehension at Time 4. This model accounted for a substantial proportion of variance in comprehension skill at thirteen to fourteen years: $R^2 = .77$.

This longitudinal study confirms the importance of a set of higher-level comprehension components that, on theoretical grounds, one would expect to be important in the growth of reading comprehension skill. In addition it is clear that early comprehension skill, and early comprehension-related skills, have far-reaching implications, and are strong predictors of comprehension skill even after six years.

IMPLICATIONS FOR ASSESSMENT

In the introduction to this chapter, we outlined how comprehension is central to reading across a wide range of materials, genres, and readers' goals. Although a range of materials may be preferable for a valid and comprehensive assessment of reading comprehension, it is not clear how to select these materials. Here, instead, we focus on what we believe is the essence of discourse comprehension: the construction of a coherent and integrated model of the meaning of the text, and the implications of our findings for the assessment of this ability.

Our work has identified some important skills for reading comprehension: inference and integration, comprehension monitoring, and knowledge and use of story structure. One important reason to consider including measures of comprehension subskills in any assessment of comprehension is that it cannot be expected that all children would have the same pattern of strengths and weaknesses.

Indeed, other work has demonstrated that less-skilled comprehenders are not a homogeneous group but have different profiles (Cornoldi, et al., 1996). For example, some less-skilled comprehenders have good vocabulary skills but poor memory or inferential skills, while others have weak vocabulary (see Cain & Oakhill, 2006). Thus, an assessment that targets a range of discourse processing skills, rather than the more commonly used general all-purpose measure of reading comprehension, has the potential to provide useful information about an individual reader's strengths and weaknesses.

However, we also need to consider the value of attempting to assess separately what are almost certainly interrelated skills. In our longitudinal work, the skills we measured predicted statistically independent portions of variance in later comprehension skill, but there are obvious reasons why they might be interlinked. For instance, comprehension monitoring cannot be entirely independent of integration skills, because the integration of information across different sentences in a text is often a requirement for spotting that there is some inconsistency between those sentences. Further, while working memory is probably supporting a reader's ability to construct a meaning-based representation of a text, it was not found to be the only determiner, and it did not predict unique variance in reading comprehension in our path analyses.

However, it might be a more important determiner of the comprehension of longer, more naturalistic, and/or more demanding texts than those used in many typical assessments of reading comprehension, such as the short texts used in the early years of our study. Indeed, working memory scores when children were aged eleven years predicted variance in the comprehension assessment administered when they were aged fourteen years, and the texts in that assessment were substantially longer. That said, the reading comprehension assessment used at Times 1-3 is highly dependent on a range of inferential skills and is not simply an assessment of memory for details (Bowyer-Crane & Snowling, 2005).

We think there are good reasons to consider these subskills separately. Along with the evidence from profiles of poor comprehenders, there is additional evidence from our longitudinal research. Other authors have also argued for the separability of these skills (Kendeou, et al., 2008). However, the relation between inference making, comprehension monitoring, story production and comprehension could be partly mediated by the reader's standard for coherence (van den Broek, Risden, & Husebye-Hartman, 1995).

For comprehension to develop satisfactorily, the reader must adopt a high standard for coherence. In other words, they must care whether the text makes sense and must strive to derive a clear, complete and coherent *situation model* of the text. When coherence is a goal, inferences are made to keep the text coherent, inconsistencies between text elements—or between text elements and the reader's knowledge—are resolved rather than ignored or not noticed, and the point and structure of the text as a whole is appreciated by the reader. These, in turn, guide and reinforce comprehension.

Given these considerations, the question of whether these subskills of comprehension should be assessed separately becomes more complex. Even though the skills, as we have argued, are necessarily interlinked to some extent, this does not mean that all children who have comprehension problems have difficulties in all areas. Indeed, it may be that a child presents with a primary deficit in one skill area, which subsequently affects other areas, and consequently some children would be more likely to benefit from different types of instruction than others (depending on their particular patterns of strengths and weaknesses).

A first step to resolving these issues would be to conduct large-scale empirical studies that systematically relate assessment of these skills to concurrent reading and listening comprehension measures. This would enable us to determine whether these subskills are identifiable *and* stable *and* independent.

Ultimately, such multifaceted assessments should be related to instruction and to instructional outcomes. If children do exhibit different profiles of strengths and weaknesses, then that might have implications for the focus of instruction. We believe that even if such subskills were not found to be independent, such an assessment of reading (and listening) comprehension would provide a more rounded and, therefore, valid assessment of what is generally acknowledged to be a complex skill.

REFERENCES

Altemeier, L. E., Abbott, R. D., & Berninger, V. W. (2008). Executive functions for reading and writing in typical literacy development and dyslexia. *Journal of Clinical and Experimental Neuropsychology, 30*, 588–606.

Baker, L. (1984). Children's effective use of multiple standards for evaluating their comprehension. *Journal of Educational Psychology, 76*, 588–97.

Barnes, M. A., Dennis, M., & Haefele-Kalvaitis, J. (1996). The effects of knowledge availability and knowledge accessibility on coherence and elaborative inferencing in children from six to fifteen years of age. *Journal of Experimental Child Psychology, 61*, 216–41.

Beal, C. R., Garrod, A. C., & Bonitatibus, G. J. (1990). Fostering children's revision skills through training in comprehension monitoring. *Journal of Educational Psychology, 82*, 275–80.

Beck, I. L. & McKeown, M. G. (1991). Social studies texts are hard to understand: Mediating some of the difficulties. *Language Arts, 68*, 482–90.

Bowyer-Crane, C., & Snowling, M. (2005). Assessing children's inference generation: What do tests of reading comprehension measure? *British Journal of Educational Psychology, 75*, 189–201.

Cain, K. (1996). Story knowledge and comprehension skill. In C. Cornoldi & J. Oakhill (Eds.), *Reading comprehension difficulties: Processes and remediation* (pp. 167–92). Mahwah, NJ: Lawrence Erlbaum Associates.

———. (2003). Text comprehension and its relation to coherence and cohesion in children's fictional narratives. *British Journal of Developmental Psychology, 21*, 335–51.

Cain, K., & Oakhill, J. (1996). The nature of the relationship between comprehension skill and the ability to tell a story. *British Journal of Developmental Psychology, 14,* 187–201.

———. (1999). Inference making and its relation to comprehension failure. *Reading and Writing, 11,* 489–503.

———. (2006). Profiles of children with specific reading comprehension difficulties. *British Journal of Educational Psychology, 76,* 683–96.

———. (2007). Reading comprehension difficulties: Correlates, causes, and consequences. In K. Cain & J. Oakhill (Eds.), *Children's comprehension problems in oral and written language: A cognitive perspective* (pp. 41–75). New York: Guilford Press.

———. (2011). Matthew effects in young readers: Do reading comprehension and reading experience aid vocabulary development? *Journal of Learning Disabilities, 44,* 431–443.

Cain, K., Oakhill, J. V., Barnes, M. A., & Bryant, P. E. (2001). Comprehension skill, inference making ability and their relation to knowledge. *Memory and Cognition, 29,* 850–59.

Cain, K., Oakhill, J. V., & Bryant, P. E. (2000a). Investigating the causes of reading comprehension failure: The comprehension-age match design. *Reading and Writing, 12,* 31–40.

———. (2000b). Phonological skills and comprehension failure: A test of the phonological processing deficit hypothesis. *Reading and Writing. An Interdisciplinary Journal, 13,* 31–56.

———. (2004). Children's reading comprehension ability: Concurrent prediction by working memory, verbal ability, and component skills. *Journal of Educational Psychology, 96,* 671–81.

Cain, K., Oakhill, J. V., & Elbro, C. (2003). The ability to learn new word meanings from context by school-age children with and without language comprehension difficulties. *Journal of Child Language, 30,* 681–94.

Cain, K., Oakhill, J. V., & Lemmon, K. (2004). Individual differences in the inference of word meanings from context: The influence of reading comprehension, vocabulary knowledge, and memory capacity. *Journal of Educational Psychology, 96,* 671–81.

Casteel, M. A. (1993). Effects of inference necessity and reading goal on children's inference generation. *Developmental Psychology, 29,* 346–57.

Catts, H. W., Adlof, S. M., & Weismer, S. E. (2006). Language deficits in poor comprehenders: A case for the simple view of reading. *Journal of Speech, Language, and Hearing Research, 49,* 278–93.

Catts, H. W., Hogan, T. P., & Fey, M. E. (2003). Subgrouping poor readers on the basis of individual differences in reading-related abilities. *Journal of Learning Disabilities, 36,* 151–64.

Cornoldi, C., de Beni, R., & Pazzaglia, F. (1996). Profiles of reading comprehension difficulties: An analysis of single cases. In C. Cornoldi & J. Oakhill (Eds.), *Reading comprehension difficulties: Processes and intervention* (pp. 113–36). Mahwah, NJ: Lawrence Erlbaum Associates.

Cragg, L., & Nation, K. (2006). Exploring written narrative in children with poor reading comprehension. *Educational Psychology, 26*, 55–72.

Cunningham, A. E., & Stanovich, K. E. (1998). What reading does for the mind. *American Educator, 22*, 8–15.

deJong, P. F. & van der Leij, A. (2002). Effects of phonological abilities and linguistic comprehension on the development of reading. *Scientific Studies of Reading, 6*, 51–77.

Dimino, J., Gersten, R., Carnine, D., & Blake, G. (1990). Story grammar: An approach for promoting at-risk secondary students' comprehension of literature. *The Elementary School Journal, 91*, 19–32.

Ehrlich, M. F. (1996). Metacognitive monitoring in the processing of anaphoric devices in skilled and less-skilled comprehenders. In C. Cornoldi & J. Oakhill (Eds.), *Reading comprehension difficulties: Processes and intervention* (pp. 221–49). Mahwah, NJ: Lawrence Erlbaum Associates.

Ehrlich, M. F., & Remond, M. (1997). Skilled and less skilled comprehenders: French children's processing of anaphoric devices in written texts. *British Journal of Developmental Psychology, 15*, 291–309.

Ehrlich, M. F., Remond, M., & Tardieu, H. (1999). Processing of anaphoric devices in young skilled and less skilled comprehenders: Differences in metacognitive monitoring. *Reading and Writing, 11*, 29–63.

Gough, P. B., & Tunmer, W. E. (1986). Decoding, reading and reading disability. *Remedial and Special Education, 7*, 6–10.

Katzir, T., Young-Suk, K., Wolf, M., Morris, R. K., & Lovett, M. W. (2008). The varieties of pathways to dysfluent reading: Comparing subtypes of children with dyslexia at letter, word, and connected text levels of reading. *Journal of Learning Disabilities, 41*, 47–66.

Kendeou, P., Bohn-Gettler, C., White, M., & van den Broek, P. (2008). Children's inference generation across different media. *Journal of Research in Reading, 31*, 259–72.

Kendeou, P., van den Broek, P., White, M., & Lynch, J. S. (2009). Predicting reading comprehension in early elementary school: The independent contributions of oral language and decoding skills. *Journal of Educational Psychology, 101*, 765–78.

Kintsch, W. (1998). *Comprehension: A paradigm for cognition.* New York: Cambridge University Press.

Long, D. L., & Chong, J. L. (2001). Comprehension skill and global coherence: A paradoxical picture of poor comprehenders' abilities. *Journal of Experimental Psychology: Learning, Memory, & Cognition, 27*, 1424–429.

Markman, E. M., & Gorin, L. (1981). Children's ability to adjust their standards for evaluating comprehension. *Journal of Educational Psychology, 73*, 320–25.

Mason, J. M. (1992). Reading stories in preliterate children: A proposed connection to reading. In P. B. Gough, L. C. Ehri & R. Treiman (Eds.), *Reading acquisition* (pp. 215–41). Hillsdale, NJ: Lawrence Erlbaum Associates.

McGee, A., & Johnson, H. (2003). The effect of inference training on skilled and less skilled comprehenders. *Educational Psychology, 23*, 49–59.

Megherbi, H., & Ehrlich, M. F. (2005). Language impairment in less skilled comprehenders: The on-line processing of anaphoric pronouns in a listening situation. *Reading and Writing, 18*, 715–53.

Mezynski, K. (1983). Issues concerning the acquisition of knowledge: Effects of vocabulary training on reading comprehension. *Review of Educational Research, 53,* 253–79.

Millis, K. K., & Graesser, A. C. (1994). The time-course of constructing knowledge-based inferences for scientific texts. *Journal of Memory and Language, 33,* 583–99.

Muter, V., Hulme, C., Snowling, M., & Stevenson, J. (2004). Phonemes, rimes, vocabulary and grammatical skills as foundations of early reading development: Evidence from a longitudinal study. *Developmental Psychology, 40,* 665–81.

Nation, K., & Snowling, M. (1999). Developmental differences in sensitivity to semantic relations among good and poor comprehenders: Evidence from semantic priming. *Cognition, 70,* 81–83.

———. (2004). Beyond phonological skills: Broader language skills contribute to the development of reading. *Journal of Research in Reading, 27,* 342–56.

Nesi, B., Levorato, M. C., Roch, M., & Cacciari, C. (2006). To break the embarrassment: text comprehension skills and figurative competence in skilled and less-skilled text comprehenders. *European Psychologist, 11,* 128–36.

Oakhill, J. V. (1982). Constructive processes in skilled and less-skilled comprehenders' memory for sentences. *British Journal of Psychology, 73,* 13–20.

———. (1984). Inferential and memory skills in children's comprehension of stories. *British Journal of Educational Psychology,* 54 31–39.

Oakhill, J. V. & Cain, K. (2012). The precursors of reading comprehension and word reading in young readers: Evidence from a four-year longitudinal study. *Scientific Studies of Reading,* 16, 91–121.

Oakhill, J. V., Hartt, J., & Samols, D. (2005). Levels of comprehension monitoring and working memory in good and poor comprehenders. *Reading and Writing, 18,* 657–713.

Ouellette, G. P. (2006). What's meaning got to do with it: The role of vocabulary in word reading and reading comprehension. *Journal of Educational Psychology, 98,* 554–66.

Paris, A. H., & Paris, S. G. (2003). Assessing narrative comprehension in young children. *Reading Research Quarterly, 38,* 36–76.

Perfetti, C. A. (1985). *Reading ability.* New York: Oxford University Press.

———. (2007). Reading ability: Lexical quality to comprehension. *Scientific Studies of Reading, 11,* 357–83.

Skarakis-Doyle, E. (2002). Young children's detection of violations in familiar stories and emerging comprehension monitoring. *Discourse Processes, 33,* 175–97.

Snowling, M. J. (2000). *Dyslexia* (2nd ed.). Oxford: Blackwell Publishing.

Speece, D. L., Roth, F. A., Cooper, D. H., & De La Paz, S. (1999). The relevance of oral language skills to early literacy: A multivariate analysis. *Applied Psycholinguistics, 20,* 167–90.

Stanovich, K. E. (1986). Matthew effects in reading: Some consequences of individual differences in the acquisition of literacy. *Reading Research Quarterly, 21,* 360–406.

———. (1993). Does reading make you smarter? Literacy and the development of verbal intelligence. In H. Reese (Ed.), *Advances in child development and behavior* (Vol. 24, pp. 133–80). San Diego: Academic Press.

Stein, N. L., & Trabasso, T. (1982). What's in a story: An approach to comprehension and instruction. In R. Glaser (Ed.), *Advances in the psychology of instruction* (Vol. 2, pp. 213–67). Hillsdale, NJ: Lawrence Erlbaum Associates.

Stothard, S. E., & Hulme, C. (1996). A comparison of phonological skills in children with reading comprehension difficulties and children with word reading difficulties. *Journal of Child Psychology and Child Psychiatry, 36,* 399–408.

Trabasso, T., & Stein, N. L. (1997). Narrating, representing, and remembering event sequences. In P. W. van den Broek, P. J. Bauer & T. Bourg (Eds.), *Developmental spans in event comprehension and representation: Bridging fictional and actual events* (pp. 237–70). Hillsdale, NJ: Lawrence Erlbaum Associate.

van den Broek, P. W., Risden, K., & Husebye-Hartman, E. (1995). The role of readers' standards for coherence in the generation of inferences during reading. In R. F. Lorch & E. J. O'Brien (Eds.), *Sources of coherence in reading* (pp. 353–73). Mahwah, NJ: Lawrence Erlbaum Associates.

Vellutino, F. R., Tunmer, W. E., Jaccard, J. J., & Chen, R. (2007). Components of reading ability: Multivariate evidence for a convergent skill model of reading development. *Scientific Studies of Reading, 11,* 3–32.

Yuill, N. M., & Oakhill, J. V. (1988). Effects of inference awareness training on poor reading comprehension. *Applied Cognitive Psychology, 2,* 33–45.

———. (1991). *Children's problems in text comprehension: An experimental investigation.* Cambridge: Cambridge University Press.

Chapter Five

Measure for Measure: Challenges in Assessing Reading Comprehension[1]

Janice M. Keenan

I borrowed from Shakespeare in titling this chapter *Measure for Measure* not only because I will be talking about the details of many measures of reading comprehension, but also to highlight a characteristic of these measures that seems very Shakespearean. Just as many of Shakespeare's characters initially appear to be one person and then later in the play are shown to be someone else, so too we have found that many reading comprehension tests are not as they appear. They are labeled as tests of comprehension, but as you will come to see in this chapter, on closer scrutiny some of them are mostly tests of word decoding skill and less tests of what we typically regard as comprehension skills. To set the *stage*, so to speak, for this claim, we begin by giving some background on our National Institutes of Health (NIH) research project that led us to these insights into reading comprehension tests.

COMPREHENSION ASSESSMENT IN THE COLORADO LEARNING DISABILITIES RESEARCH CENTER

Children differ in how quickly they learn to read and how readily they comprehend what they read. The focus of our work in the Reading and Language Lab at the University of Denver has been to understand why. What causes these individual differences to develop? How are the cognitive processes different? What are ways to help those who have deficits?

We are part of a team of researchers called the Colorado Learning Disabilities Research Center (http://ibgwww.colorado.edu/cldrc/index.html), which is one of four research centers funded by the NIH to study learning disabilities (cf., DeFries et al., 1997; Olson, 2006). We study twins because

twins allow us to separate the influences of genes and environments on behavior. My focus is on reading comprehension. By comparing the similarities
of identical twins to those of fraternal twins, we are gaining insights into the
etiology of individual differences in reading comprehension and investigating the extent to which component skills of comprehension share a common
genetic basis or whether there are independent genetic influences associated
with each (Keenan, Betjemann, Wadsworth, DeFries, & Olson, 2006).

Because comprehension had not previously been studied separately from
word reading with behavioral genetic methods, we designed our test battery
to include extensive testing of reading comprehension as well as listening
comprehension, using several standardized tests as well as our own experimental measures.

Our use of multiple tests has given us the unique opportunity to examine
how similarly the same child performs across these different measures of
reading comprehension. To our surprise, we found that intercorrelations
among our tests were rather modest (Keenan, Betjemann, & Olson, 2008).
Thus, despite the tendency in both clinical practice and research to treat tests
of reading comprehension as interchangeable, our data suggest they are not.

When we explored the reasons underlying the modest correlations among
our reading comprehension tests, we found there were dramatic differences
among the tests in the amount of variance accounted for by word decoding skill. The only previous comparison of tests of reading comprehension
used in the United States (Cutting & Scarborough, 2006) had found some
minor differences among the Gates-MacGinitie Reading Test (GMRT), the
Wechsler Individual Achievement Test (WIAT), and the Gray Oral Reading
Test (GORT) in the amount of variance accounted for by word decoding skill.

The differences we uncovered in our tests, however, were much larger;
we even found that the relative influence of decoding versus comprehension
skill in explaining reading comprehension reverses across tests. Because our
fortuitous choice of reading comprehension tests showed such big differences
among the tests and even within the same test depending on the child's age, it
permitted new insights into the nature of reading comprehension assessment.

In this chapter we describe these insights. Our goal is not so much to make
claims about the validity of specific reading comprehension tests. Rather,
it is to learn from analyzing test differences what the factors are that might
contribute to making performance on some tests heavily dependent on decoding skill, while performance on others much less so. Can we identify aspects
of the test format that might be responsible? Or is it the type of information
queried by these tests? Another goal is to examine how characteristics of the
reader, in particular developmental level, lead the test to be more a test of
word identification skill than comprehension skill.

HOW DO READING COMPREHENSION
TESTS VARY IN THE SKILLS THEY ASSESS?

The goal of reading comprehension tests is to assess the cognitive skills involved in understanding texts beyond the skill of word decoding. We know from groundbreaking work by Oakhill, Cain, and others that there is independence between decoding and comprehension skills because they have identified children who have problems in reading comprehension despite adequate word reading skill (Cain & Oakhill, 2007; Catts, Hogan, & Fey, 2003; Nation, 2005; Oakhill, 1994; Perfetti, Landi, & Oakhill, 2005; Yuill & Oakhill, 1991).

We have recently shown that this independence has a biological basis (Keenan et al., 2006); we have found that separate sets of genes underlie word recognition and listening comprehension because each accounts for significant independent genetic influences on reading comprehension, although there is also considerable shared genetic variance among them. Given the genetic and cognitive separability of these two components, it is important that our assessments of reading comprehension assess both.

In Keenan et al. (2008), our method for comparing reading comprehension tests was to use composites of twins' performance on word decoding tests and tests of listening comprehension (the listening tests assessed comprehending discourse ranging from short passages to long stories) to account for the variance in each of our reading comprehension tests. The reading comprehension tests we compared are the *Gray Oral Reading Test–3* (GORT) (Wiederholt & Bryant, 1992), the *Qualitative Reading Inventory–3* (QRI) (Leslie & Caldwell, 2001), the *Woodcock-Johnson Passage Comprehension* subtest (WJPC) from the Woodcock-Johnson Tests of Achievement-III (Woodcock, McGrew, & Mather, 2001), and the Reading Comprehension subtest from the *Peabody Individual Achievement Test* (PIAT) (Dunn & Markwardt, 1970), which is identical in format to the PIAT-R and PIAT-R/NU (Markwardt, 1989; 1997).

These reading comprehension tests were selected because they represent a range of test format options, summarized in Table 5.1. Two tests are silent reading (WJPC and PIAT), and two are oral reading (GORT and QRI). Passage length varies from a single sentence (PIAT and most WJPC texts) to long passages up to 785 words (QRI). The tasks used to assess comprehension vary from selecting a picture that best represents the meaning of each sentence in the PIAT to the cloze (fill in the blank) technique in the WJPC, to multiple-choice comprehension questions in the GORT and open-ended comprehension questions and retellings in the QRI. The sample consisted of 510 individuals between the ages of eight and eighteen. All had English as

Table 5.1.   Format features of our reading comprehension tests

Gray Oral Reading Test (GORT):
- *Oral Reading*
- *Passage Length* = Multiple-Sentence Texts (118 words on average)
- *Comprehension Assessment:* Multiple-Choice Comprehension Questions

Peabody Individual Achievement Test (PIAT):
- *Silent Reading*
- *Passage Length* = Single Sentence
- *Comprehension Assessment:* Multiple-Choice Picture Selection

Qualitative Reading Inventory (QRI):
- *Oral Reading*
- *Passage Length* = Long Multiple-Sentence Texts (360 words on average)
- *Comprehension Assessment:* Open-Ended, Short Answer Comprehension Questions
- *Comprehension Assessment:* Retelling of Passage

Woodcock-Johnson Passage Comprehension Test (WJPC):
- *Silent Reading*
- *Passage Length* = mostly Single Sentence; some Two-Sentence Texts
- *Comprehension Assessment:* Cloze Test (fill in the blank)

their first language, no uncorrected sensory deficits, and full-scale IQ greater than 85.

A pair of hierarchical regressions was run for each of the five reading comprehension tests to determine how much of the variance in performance on each test was accounted for uniquely by word decoding and listening comprehension and how much was shared variance. It was found that word decoding, not listening comprehension, accounts for most of the variance in performance on both the PIAT and the WJPC. Of the 59 percent of the variance accounted for in the PIAT, less than 5 percent was uniquely accounted for by listening comprehension skills; with the WJPC, it was less than 7 percent of the 61 percent total variance.

The *reverse* pattern was found for the GORT and both QRI measures: less than 5 percent of the variance on the QRI measures and less than 7 percent on the GORT was uniquely accounted for by word decoding skill. In sum, there were dramatic differences across tests in how much individual differences in word decoding and listening comprehension skills explain individual differences in reading comprehension.

Why Do Some Reading Comprehension Tests Assess Mostly Word Decoding?

What factors might contribute to making performance on reading comprehension tests more reflective of decoding skill than comprehension skills? Is it something about the format? Previous research has suggested that cloze tests differ from other comprehension tests in that most of the variance in cloze tests is accounted for by decoding skill (Nation & Snowling, 1997; Francis, Fletcher, Catts, & Tomblin, 2005).

What we found, however, is that the PIAT, which uses multiple-choice selection of pictures representing the meaning of the sentence, showed the same pattern as the WJPC's cloze-test format. Thus, it is not just the cloze test format that leads to a comprehension test primarily reflecting decoding. Some other factor seems responsible. We think there are good reasons to assume that this factor is passage length. Short texts lead to assessing mainly decoding skill.

There are two reasons why comprehension assessments of short texts end up being mainly assessments of decoding skill. One is that failure to decode just a single word can be catastrophic to understanding when a passage consists of only a single sentence. If a child cannot determine whether a word is *magician* or *musician*, there is typically no way for him or her to resolve this when the text is a single sentence. If the comprehension assessment requires the child then to pick among pictures involving magicians and musicians or fill in the blank with a word that would be relevant to magician, he or she will appear to have not understood the sentence, when in fact all the child failed to do was identify one word.

When tests use passages longer than a sentence, however, then the passage may continue by referring to events that resolve the identity of the unknown word. For example, the passage may describe taking a rabbit out of a hat. In sum, longer passages provide sufficient context to make comprehension robust to decoding failures.

Another reason why comprehension assessments of short texts end up being mainly assessments of decoding skill is that when there are so few words and ideas, as in a short single-sentence passage, there is not much to assess. As a result, the assessment of understanding, whether it is a cloze test or any other format, is likely to be based on a single word. Although what is typically meant by comprehension is the integration of ideas, when a text presents only one idea, there is no integration to assess. Longer passages are needed to permit the assessment of integration of ideas and to minimize the possibility of decoding failures preventing assessment of comprehension processes.

In the Keenan et al. (2008) study, both the GORT and the QRI had relatively little of their variance explained by word decoding skill compared to the PIAT and the WJPC. The previous discussion may suggest that the reason is that both tests use longer passages. It is true that both use longer passages, with the QRI passages being the longest.

However, there is a different reason why word decoding skill has so little influence on the GORT: It is the passage independence of the test items.

As we reported in Keenan and Betjemann (2006), most (86 percent) of the GORT multiple-choice questions can be answered with above-chance accuracy without even reading the passages. In fact, the best predictor of performance on GORT comprehension questions is not how accurately one reads the passages, but rather how easily the question can be answered by people who have not read the passage.

Unfortunately, this is not a problem unique to the GORT. Coleman, Lindstrom, Nelson, Lindstrom, & Gregg (2010) have reported a similar problem with a test used with college students, the Nelson-Denny reading test. This problem of passage-independence of comprehension questions points to yet another challenge in developing assessments of reading comprehension.

DEVELOPMENTAL DIFFERENCES AMONG TESTS

When decoding skills are weaker, as in younger children or in children with specific deficits in word reading, we expect to find that decoding will account for more variance in reading comprehension than it does in older children (Catts, Hogan, & Adolf, 2005; Curtis, 1980). What we do not expect to find is that tests of reading comprehension will be differentially affected by this. But that is exactly what we found in Keenan et al. (2008).

We found that age (both chronological age as well as reading age defined as word reading level) interacts with decoding as a function of test, with the interaction significantly larger for the PIAT and WJPC than the other tests (Keenan et al., 2008). In other words, there are developmental differences in what a test is measuring depending on both age and reading ability. When the comprehension test is mainly a test of word decoding skill, like the PIAT and the WJPC, what is being assessed by the test switches as children get older and their decoding skill approaches a ceiling. Thus, for less skilled and younger readers, we find that the PIAT and WJPC are more assessments of decoding skill, whereas for more advanced readers, these tests reflect some listening comprehension skills.

In contrast, the QRI and the GORT did not show significant differences across age groups in what is assessed because these comprehension tests are more of comprehension than word decoding skill.

These developmental test differences have serious implications for interpreting our assessments. For one thing, the assumption that reading comprehension tests are comparable and interchangeable appears especially erroneous for assessing younger children's comprehension skills. There are greater differences between what reading comprehension tests are measuring when children are younger or less skilled than when they are older.

Another implication is for longitudinal assessment when the same test is used to chart progress in reading. If that test is one where what is being assessed changes depending on developmental level, then it is difficult to interpret longitudinal changes. For example, a child whose standard scores decline across testing time points may indeed be declining; alternatively, the child may be manifesting a deficit in comprehension skills that had been there all along but had not been detected earlier because earlier tests of reading comprehension mainly assessed word decoding skill, not comprehension skill.

HOW PRIOR KNOWLEDGE DIFFERENCES MAY IMPACT COMPREHENSION ASSESSMENT

Beginning with Bransford and Johnson's (1972) seminal study, many researchers have shown that having some prior knowledge about the topic of a passage enables both greater comprehension of the text and better memory for it (McNamara & Kintsch, 1996; Rawson & Kintsch, 2004; Rawson & Van Overschelde, 2008; Spilich, Vesonder, Chiesi, & Voss, 1979). Having prior familiarity with and knowledge of objects and events referred to by the words in the text allows the reader to easily construct a mental model of the situation being described.

One of the things we have found in our work with children who have word reading deficits is how helpful prior domain knowledge can be. When word reading is not fluent and automatic, it requires more cognitive resources. What we have found is that the effect of more resources being diverted to word recognition means that their comprehension suffers.

Unfortunately, what suffers above all is comprehension of the most central information. We have termed this the "centrality deficit" (Miller & Keenan, 2009). What is exciting, however, is that Miller and Keenan showed that having prior knowledge can compensate for the reduced comprehension resources that children with reading disability have: poor readers with prior topic knowledge do not show the centrality deficit that occurs in these children when they lack that prior knowledge. We have also found that prior knowledge can facilitate passage fluency and the semantic appropriateness of word substitutions in oral reading (Priebe, Keenan, & Miller, 2012).

The effects of prior knowledge on comprehension are so pronounced and its compensatory properties for children with word reading problems so promising that it suggests we need to think about taking prior knowledge into account when interpreting outcomes of reading comprehension tests. Although it is true that there can be children who will continue to show comprehension deficits even when they are equated with controls on prior background knowledge (Barnes, Dennis, & Haefele-Kalvaitis, 1996; Cain, Oakhill, Barnes, & Bryant, 2001), our work suggests that the difference between good and poor readers could often lie solely in their familiarity with the topic of the passage.

All the research on prior knowledge and comprehension tell us that a child who has had opportunities to go to aquariums and view picture books of sea life will be able to comprehend a passage about manatees more readily than a child who has not. Yet often when we interpret scores on comprehension tests, we are inclined to view lower performance as reflecting deficits in comprehension skills when it could simply reflect unfamiliarity with the topic. A promising approach to reading comprehension assessment in the twenty-first century thus would be to incorporate prior knowledge assessment into comprehension assessment and attempt to assess children's comprehension skills both when they are familiar with a topic and when they are not (cf., Pearson & Hamm, 2005).

CONCLUSION

We began this chapter by drawing a parallel between some reading comprehension tests and some Shakespearean characters who masquerade as one thing and are later shown to be another. We have presented a number of findings that suggest that some masquerading happens in reading assessment as well.

One can question the appropriateness of the label "reading comprehension test" when a test is such that most of its questions can be answered correctly without even reading (Keenan & Betjemann, 2006), or when variance on the tests is mostly explained by word decoding skill, not comprehension (Keenan, et al., 2008). These are problems of content validity, and we hope that the standardized testing industry will take it as a wakeup call rather than treating it as much ado about nothing (to continue the Shakespearean references of this chapter).

We think there are many conclusions here that can be used to shape reading comprehension assessment in the twenty-first century. One is a renewed appreciation for the complexity of our task. As we have uncovered the many differences among tests, and even within the same test depending on the age of the child, we realize that the more complex the construct, the more likely that there will be differences across instruments in how they tap into those skills. Reading comprehension tests are not as interchangeable as word reading tests.

Another conclusion is to ensure that future reading comprehension tests do more than function as tests of word identification skill or vocabulary, but test the integration of ideas and the construction of an interpretation. Finally, we hope that there will be recognition of the role of prior knowledge in comprehension so that future reading comprehension tests will assess comprehension both in domains for which children have knowledge as well as those in which they do not.

REFERENCES

Barnes, M. A., Dennis, M., & Haefele-Kalvaitis, J. (1996). The effects of knowledge availability and knowledge accessibility on coherence and elaborative inferencing in children from six to fifteen years of age. *Journal of Experimental Child Psychology, 61*, 216–41.

Bransford, J., & Johnson, M. (1972). Contextual prerequisites for understanding: Some investigations of comprehension and recall. *Journal of Verbal Learning & Verbal Behavior, 11*, 717–26.

Cain, K., & Oakhill, J. (2007). Reading comprehension difficulties: Correlates, causes, and consequences. In K. Cain & J. Oakhill (Eds.), *Children's comprehension problems in oral and written language* (pp. 41–75). New York: The Guilford Press.

Cain, K., Oakhill, J. V., Barnes, M. A., & Bryant, P. E. (2001). Comprehension skill, inference making ability and their relation to knowledge. *Memory & Cognition, 29*, 850–59.

Catts, H. W., Hogan, T. P., & Adolf, S. M. (2005). Developmental changes in reading and reading disabilities. In Catts, H. W., & Kamhi, A. G. (Eds.), Language and reading disabilities (pp. 25–40). Boston: Allyn & Bacon.

Catts, H. W., Hogan, T. P., & Fey, M. E. (2003). Subgrouping poor readers on the basis of individual differences in reading-related abilities. *Journal of Learning Disabilities, 36*, 151–64.

Coleman, C., Lindstrom, J. H., Nelson, J. M., Lindstrom, W., & Gregg, N. (2010). Passageless comprehension on the Nelson-Denny reading test: Well above chance for university students. *Journal of Learning Disabilities, 43*, 244–49.

Curtis, M. E. (1980). Development of components of reading skill. *Journal of Educational Psychology, 72*, 656–69.

Cutting, L. E., & Scarborough, H. S. (2006). Prediction of reading comprehension: Relative contributions of word recognition, language proficiency, and other cognitive skills can depend on how comprehension is measured. *Scientific Studies of Reading, 10*, 277–99.

DeFries, J. C., Filipek, P. A., Fulker, D. W., Olson, R. K., Pennington, B. F., & Smith, S. D. (1997). Colorado Learning Disabilities Research Center. *Learning Disabilities, 8*, 7–19.

Dunn, L. M., & Markwardt, F. C. (1970). *Examiner's manual: Peabody Individual Achievement Test.* Circle Pines, MN: American Guidance Service.

Francis, D. J., Fletcher, J. M., Catts, H.W., & Tomblin, J. B. (2005). Dimensions affecting the assessment of reading comprehension. In S. G. Paris & S. A. Stahl (Eds.), *Children's reading comprehension and assessment* (pp. 369–94). Mahwah, NJ: Lawrence Erlbaum Associates.

Keenan, J. M., & Betjemann, R. S. (2006). Comprehending the Gray Oral Reading Test without reading it: Why comprehension tests should not include passage-independent items. *Scientific Studies of Reading, 10,* 363–80.

Keenan, J. M., Betjemann, R. S., & Olson, R. K. (2008). Reading comprehension tests vary in the skills they assess: Differential dependence on decoding and oral comprehension. *Scientific Studies of Reading, 12,* 281–300.

Keenan, J. M., Betjemann, R. S., Wadsworth, S. J., DeFries, J. C., & Olson, R.K. (2006). Genetic and environmental influences on reading and listening comprehension. *Journal of Research in Reading, 29,* 79–91.

Leslie, L., & Caldwell, J. (2001). *Qualitative Reading Inventory–3.* New York: Addison Wesley Longman, Inc.

Markwardt, F. C. (1989; 1997 Normative Update). *Peabody Individual Achievement Test–Revised.* Bloomington, MN: Pearson Assessments.

McNamara, D.S., & Kintsch, W. (1996). Learning from texts: Effects of prior knowledge and text coherence. *Discourse Processes, 22,* 247–82.

Miller, A. C., & Keenan, J. M. (2009). How word decoding skill impacts text memory: The centrality deficit and how domain knowledge can compensate. *Annals of Dyslexia, 59,* 99–113.

Nation, K. (2005). Children's reading comprehension difficulties. In M. Snowling & C. Hulme (Eds.), *The science of reading: A handbook* (pp. 248–65). Oxford: Blackwell.

Nation, K., & Snowling, M. (1997). Assessing reading difficulties: The validity and utility of current measures of reading skill. *British Journal of Educational Psychology, 67,* 359–70.

Oakhill, J., (1994). Individual differences in children's text comprehension. In M. A. Gernsbacher (Ed.), *Handbook of psycholinguistics* (pp. 821–48). San Diego: Academic.

Olson, R.K. (2006). Genes, environment, and dyslexia: The 2005 Norman Geschwind memorial lecture. *Annals of Dyslexia, 56,* 205–38.

Pearson, P., & Hamm, D. (2005). The assessment of reading comprehension: A review of practices-past, present, and future. In S. G. Paris & S. A. Stahl (Eds.), *Children's reading comprehension and assessment* (pp. 13–69). Mahwah, NJ: Lawrence Erlbaum Associates.

Perfetti, C. A., Landi, N., & Oakhill, J. (2005). The acquisition of reading comprehension skill. In M. Snowling & C. Hulme (Eds.), *The science of reading: A handbook* (pp. 227–47). Oxford: Blackwell.

Priebe, S. J., Keenan, J. M., & Miller, A. C. (2012). How prior knowledge affects word identification and comprehension. *Reading and Writing, 25,* 131–149.

Rawson, K. A., & Kintsch, W. (2004). Exploring encoding and retrieval effects of background information on text memory. *Discourse Processes, 38*, 323–44.

Rawson, K. A., & Van Overschelde, J. P. (2008). How does knowledge promote memory? The distinctiveness theory of skilled memory. *Journal of Memory and Language, 58*, 646–68.

Spilich, G., Vesonder, G., Chiesi, H., & Voss, J. (1979). Text processing of domain-related information for individuals with high and low domain knowledge. *Journal of Verbal Learning & Verbal Behavior, 18*, 275–90.

Wiederholt, L., & Bryant, B. (1992). *Examiner's manual: Gray Oral Reading Test–3.* Austin, TX: Pro-Ed.

Woodcock, R. W., McGrew, K. S., & Mather, N. (2001). *Woodcock-Johnson III Tests of Achievement.* Itasca, IL: Riverside Publishers.

Yuill, N. M., & Oakhill, J. V. (1991). *Children's problems in text comprehension: An experimental investigation.* Cambridge UK: Cambridge University Press.

NOTE

1. This research was supported by a grant from the National Institute of Child & Human Development P50 HD27802 to the Colorado Learning Disabilities Research Center (CLDRC), for which the author is a co-principal investigator. Thanks to all my co-PIs, the graduate students in the Reading & Language Lab at the University of Denver, all the participants and their families, and all the testers and scorers.

Chapter Six

Sources of Text Difficulty: Across Genres and Grades

Danielle S. McNamara, Arthur Graesser,
& Max Louwerse

The overarching goal of this chapter is to provide a better understanding of the characteristics of text as they vary across genres and grade levels. We regard this as a first step toward creating reading assessments for which the nature of the passages is more fully understood.

Research has shown that text cohesion is an important facet of text difficulty and that the effects of text cohesion depend on the readers' domain knowledge and reading skill. The current study further investigates the importance of text cohesion and other signatures of text difficulty by examining the characteristics of a corpus of texts that vary in grade level and text genre.

The results show that referential cohesion increases across grade levels. However, while lower-grade texts have lower referential cohesion, they have higher verb cohesion. This suggests that the smaller overlap in objects is compensated by larger overlap in actions. The results collectively point to a tradeoff between difficulty at the lexical and cohesion levels. Such a result suggests that it is insufficient to define text difficulty simply on the basis of word frequency, word length, and sentence length. Text difficulty is also a result of cohesion.

There are many issues to consider when developing measures to assess text comprehension. Most traditional reading comprehension assessments comprise brief passages that cover a relatively wide range of topics (e.g., Nelson-Denny, Gates MacGinitie tests). This breadth of coverage is assumedly intended to reduce the effects of prior knowledge on performance.

Choosing a readability range for the passages and then writing test items to the passage along some construct model (e.g., main idea, detail, reasoning, etc.) is considered state-of-the-art in test design. The assumption is that text difficulty is a unidimensional construct, most often reflected by a readability score (e.g., Flesch Reading Ease, Flesch-Kincaid, Lexile). Test designers often include a range of texts that vary in terms of difficulty according to these scores, with the assumption that by including a range of texts, the issue of text difficulty works itself out.

If the test designer is interested in creating an overall metric related to comprehension ability, using a range of texts with varying topics and readability levels may be successful. However, if the test designer's goal is to develop formative assessments that can identify specific weaknesses and strengths of readers (Magliano, Millis, Ozuru, & McNamara, 2007; VanderVeen et al., 2007), then understanding the characteristics of each particular passage is crucial. In that case, designing successful formative reading ability assessments will require understanding the passage characteristics as well as understanding how readers with varying levels of background knowledge and reading skills will be differentially affected by those text characteristics.

But what is it that makes a text difficult? Text difficulty has been gauged for almost sixty years by *readability* measures (Flesch, 1948). Such measures include Flesch Reading Ease, Flesch-Kincaid Grade Level (Klare, 1974–75), Degrees of Reading Power (DRP; Koslin, Zeno, & Koslin, 1987), and Lexile scores (Stenner, 1996).

These measures are all based on or highly correlated with two variables: the frequency or familiarity of the words, and the length or syntactic complexity of the sentences. Because frequent words tend to be short and infrequent words long, many readability measures use word length (i.e., number of letters or syllables) as an index for word frequency. Thus, many measures are based simply on word and sentence length.

Certainly, word and sentence length have considerable validity as indices of text difficulty. Longer sentences are more difficult to process and less frequent words tend to be less familiar. However, word and sentence length alone explain only a part of text comprehension and ignore many language and discourse features that have been shown to be influential at estimating comprehension difficulty (Graesser, Gernsbacher, & Goldman, 2003).

In discourse psychology, many of these features are captured by the notion of cohesion, the linguistic glue that links together the events and concepts conveyed within a text. Many studies, across a variety of paradigms and dependent measures, have shown that cohesive cues in text facilitate reading comprehension and help readers construct more coherent mental representations of text content (Britton & Gulgoz, 1991; McNamara, 2001; Zwaan & Radvansky, 1998).

Cohesion arises from a variety of sources, including explicit referential overlap and causal relationships, and can operate between sentences, groups of sentences, paragraphs, and chapters (Givón, 1995; Graesser, McNamara,

& Louwerse, 2003; Kintsch, 1998). For instance, referential cohesion refers to the degree to which there is overlap or repetition of words or concepts across sentences, paragraphs, or the entire text. Causal cohesion refers to the degree to which causal relationships are expressed explicitly, most often using connectives (e.g., *because, so,* and *therefore)* as linguistic cues. These are only two of many sources of cohesion, but they are the most widely investigated in psychological studies of discourse processing.

Cohesion differs from coherence in that cohesion is an explicit property of the text, whereas coherence refers to the quality of the mental representation constructed by a reader (Graesser, McNamara, & Louwerse, 2003; Louwerse & Graesser, 2003). It is intuitively compelling to assume that cohesion should benefit all readers. Indeed, many studies have shown that cohesion facilitates comprehension for many readers (Gernsbacher, 1990; Zwaan & Radvansky, 1998).

However, cohesion affects comprehension for different readers in different ways. For instance, cohesion is particularly crucial for low-knowledge readers (McNamara, Kintsch, Songer, & Kintsch, 1996; McNamara & Kintsch, 1996). Often when there is a lack of referential or causal cohesion, an idea, relationship, or event must be inferred by the reader. Low-knowledge readers lack the world knowledge needed to make these inferences. They often lack sufficient knowledge to interpret explicit text constituents and make the inferences needed to meaningfully connect the constituents.

When it comes to lower cohesion, however, the story is quite different for high-knowledge readers. Whereas low-knowledge readers are unable to generate inferences to fill in the conceptual gaps in the texts, high-knowledge readers are more likely to successfully do so. High-knowledge readers benefit from cohesion gaps because they are forced to generate more inferences and have sufficient knowledge to generate meaningful inferences (McNamara, 2001; McNamara & Kintsch, 1996; O'Reilly & McNamara, 2007). Successfully generating inferences aids memory and learning because prior knowledge and the information in the text are more likely to be connected in the readers' mental representation of the text, and the representation is likely to be more coherent.

Thus, text cohesion is not perfectly correlated with the reader's success in building a coherent mental representation. Nonetheless, the overwhelming evidence that cohesion aids comprehension for low-knowledge readers presents a problem for our educational system. If many texts used in classrooms are low in cohesion, and if many students do not have sufficient background knowledge, then there is a high likelihood that many students will not understand what they are asked to read.

This is likely to result because they lack the knowledge necessary to fill in the conceptual gaps, and they lack sufficient reading comprehension strategies to compensate for knowledge deficits (e.g., McNamara, 2004). Thus, assessing the cohesion of text is crucial for understanding how a reader can cope with or take advantage of cohesive cues in various types of texts (e.g., narrative, science, social studies).

Evaluating the significance of this problem requires a satisfactory objective measurement of text cohesion. This has been one of the principal objectives in the Coh-Metrix project (cohmetrix.memphis.edu). The notion that cohesion plays an important role in the comprehension processes in readers was the primary motivation for our developing the Coh-Metrix computational tool (Graesser, McNamara, Louwerse, & Cai, 2004).

Coh-Metrix is a tool that provides numerous indices of language automatically. Coh-Metrix automates indices of text cohesion to enhance more accurate measures of text difficulty. This tool augments conventional readability formulas, such as the Flesch-Kincaid and Flesch Reading Ease, with computational indices of text cohesion as well as an assortment of characteristics of words, sentences, and discourse. Coh-Metrix uses lexicons, part-of-speech classifiers, syntactic parsers, Latent Semantic Analysis (a statistical representation of world knowledge based on corpus analyses), and several other components that are widely used in computational linguistics.

For example, the Medical Research Council (MRC) database is used for psycholinguistic information about words (Coltheart, 1981). WordNet has linguistic and semantic features of words, as well as semantic relations between words (Miller, Beckwith, Fellbaum, Gross & Miller, 1990). Latent Semantic Analysis computes the semantic similarities among words, sentences, and paragraphs (Landauer & Dumais, 1997; Landauer, McNamara, Dennis, & Kintsch, 2007). Syntax is analyzed by syntactic parsers, such as Apple Pie (Sekine & Grishman, 1995) and Charniak's parser (Charniak, 2000), whereas the Brill (1992) part-of-speech tagger identifies the syntactic classes of words, including unknown words on the basis of syntactic context. Graesser et al. (2004) provide an extensive overview of the many language features provided. Coh-Metrix currently analyzes texts on three major categories of cohesion: coreference, conceptual (LSA), and connectives.

A number of studies have used Coh-Metrix to distinguish between different types of texts. For example, Louwerse, McCarthy, McNamara, and Graesser (2004) used Coh-Metrix to identify significant differences between spoken and written samples of English. McCarthy, Lewis, Dufty, and McNamara (2006) demonstrated that Coh-Metrix could successfully detect authorship even though individual authors recorded significant shifts in their writing style.

McCarthy, Briner, Rus, and McNamara (2007) showed that Coh-Metrix could distinguish between the sections that comprise typical science texts, such as *introductions, methods, results,* and *discussions.* McCarthy, Lightman, Dufty, and McNamara (2006) used Coh-Metrix to distinguish the *beginnings, middles,* and *ends* of chapters in a corpus of history and science textbooks for high school. Hall, McCarthy, Lewis, Lee, and McNamara (2007) used Coh-Metrix to distinguish a corpus of American-English law texts from a corpus of British-English law texts. In sum, Coh-Metrix has been applied to a wide variety of text corpora for the purpose of distinguishing text types.

The purpose of this study was to examine differences among the types of texts that would likely be used in reading ability tests. We examined differences between narrative texts and expository texts. Narrative texts are more easily understood than expository texts. For instance, narrative texts are read nearly twice as fast as expository texts (Graesser, Hoffman, & Clark, 1980; Haberlandt & Graesser, 1985) but recalled nearly twice as well (Graesser, Hauft-Smith, Cohen, & Pyles, 1980).

Narrative texts are more likely to convey life experiences, person-oriented dialogue, and familiar language in the oral tradition than are expository texts (Bruner, 1986; Rubin, 1995; Tonjes, Wolpow, & Zintz, 1999). In contrast, the purpose of expository texts is to inform the reader of new information. Thus, they tend to include less familiar concepts and words and require more inferences on the part of the reader. Consequently, expository texts generally demand more knowledge that fewer people have. In contrast, narrative texts are assumed to use high-frequency words.

While these differences are widely accepted, they are not fully understood. Thus, differences in word frequency, language, and cohesion between narrative and expository text need to be more systematically documented.

We have chosen three genres in this study to represent a gradient between narrative and expository texts, using language arts, social studies, and science texts. The distinction between the genres is not always clear-cut. Language arts is primarily narrative in form, but many narratives include discussions of scientific concepts and issues related to social studies, such as history, government, and politics. Science texts perhaps exemplify the genre of expository texts. Yet, many science texts and social studies texts can be written using a narrative genre. Indeed, social studies texts are somewhat of a mixed bag (e.g., history is like narrative and social studies is like expository).

We posit that the categories we included (narrative, social studies, and science) provide a gradient between the narrative and expository genres, rather than mutually exclusive categories.

If writers tend to write with their readers in mind and are considerate of them, we can assume that expository texts would be more cohesive than narratives. A good author would ideally use cohesive devices to alleviate some of the knowledge demands exerted by the expository texts. In contrast, if the necessary knowledge were readily available by most readers, the goal of captivating a reader's attention and increasing deeper comprehension would actually require reducing the cohesion of a text, to force the reader to generate inferences while reading (McNamara et al., 1996).

A counterintuitive recommendation would be quite conceivable: Writers of texts on familiar topics might be encouraged to write less cohesively so that the reader actively generates a more coherent mental representation of the text. Narrative text is one prominent instance of familiar content depicting everyday experiences, so there might be advantages in reducing cohesion. Of course, we are treating narrative quite globally and recognize that there are going to be large differences in the number and types of cohesive elements used by writers. However, our goal is to examine whether narrative text tends to exhibit different properties of cohesion than does expository text.

We also examined how texts in the genre of social studies differ from science texts. We assume that social studies texts are more like narratives in the depiction of human experiences and commonly known concepts, but more like science texts in the use of cohesive elements to didactically explain the content. That is, if the reader is assumed to be reading to learn new information, then the writer should use more cohesive elements in the text to aid the reader.

In addition to these genre differences, this study also investigated variations in text characteristics as a function of grade level. We would expect those variables associated with word familiarity (e.g., word age of acquisition, concreteness, frequency) to be highly correlated with grade level.

Our primary interest in this study, however, lies in the role of cohesion. One observation has been that texts for younger readers tend to leave out cohesive elements in order to reduce the length of the sentence and words. By consequence, this reduces the grade level estimate of the text. However, younger readers are those who have relatively less knowledge about what they are reading, regardless of the genre of the text. Thus, they should be in more need of cohesive elements. On the other hand, we can expect that when grade level estimates are lower, that cohesion should also be lower by virtue of having shorter sentences with fewer connectives. This leads to the provocative implication that younger children will be faced with less cohesive texts.

CORPUS

The purpose of this study was to examine variations in Coh-Metrix indices as a function of genre and grade level of the text. We analyzed a large corpus of texts created by the Touchstone Applied Science Associates (TASA), Inc.

The TASA corpus has nine genres consisting of 119,627 paragraphs taken from 37,651 samples. The passages all consisted of one paragraph because paragraph breaks are not marked in the TASA corpus. We focused on narrative, social studies, and science texts, which constituted the largest samples in TASA.

The TASA corpus includes the grade level for the texts as indexed by the Degrees of Reading Power (DRP) (Koslin et al., 1987). DRP tests are group-administered cloze tests consisting of nonfiction paragraphs and passages on various topics. Students are given multiple-choice options and asked to select the correct word for deleted ones in the passages. Results for the DRP are expressed in DRP scores ranging from 15– to 99+. These represent the difficulty of materials that students can read. For texts that are tested, the DRP scores are indicative of the reading level of the student required to obtain 75 percent correct on the cloze tests.

For the texts in the TASA corpus, however, DRP grade level is defined by a formula that includes word and sentence characteristics, such as word frequency and sentence length. We first divided the texts into twelve categories of grade levels based on the DRP scores in the TASA corpus. The grade levels and their DRP ranges for these twelve levels are provided in Table 6.1.

We randomly chose 100 passages from each of the 3 genres and each of the 12 grade levels, for a total of 3,600 passages. To simplify the data analysis and presentation, grade level was then collapsed across grades 1 to 3, 4 to 6, 7 to 9, and 10 to 12. We refer to these as grades 2, 5, 8, and 11. The average

Table 6.1. Ranges of the DRP scores as a function of grade level categories

Collapsed Grade	Grade	DRP Ranges	
		Minimum	Maximum
	Grade 1	35.377	45.990
Grade 2	Grade 2	46.021	48.973
	Grade 3	49.017	50.999
	Grade 4	51.001	52.995
Grade 5	Grade 5	53.010	55.998
	Grade 6	56.001	58.984
	Grade 7	59.004	59.999
Grade 8	Grade 8	60.008	61.000
	Grade 9	61.001	61.998
	Grade 10	62.000	63.999
Grade 11	Grade 11	64.013	65.997
	Grade 12	66.003	66.998

DRP scores by grade category were 46.97, 54.72, 60.49, and 64.84, respectively. We verified that the effects of grade were linear for all of the variables of interest. Thus, collapsing the data allows us to more easily present the data without loss of information.

Results and Discussion

For each of the indices of interest, an Analysis of Variance (ANOVA) was conducted that factorially varied the between-text variables: genre (narrative, social studies, science) and DRP grade level (2, 5, 8, 11). All of the indices discussed here showed significant differences as a function of genre and grade. Indeed, the probability values were rarely greater (or less significant) than .0001. Therefore, the probability values corresponding to the F values are provided only when it is greater than .01. Both Tukey HSD and Bonferroni tests of significance were conducted to interpret significant differences.

Our main interest is on differences in cohesion as a function of genre, but we are also interested in how those differences vary as a function of DRP grade level (or sentence and word complexity).

Descriptive and Readability Statistics

Table 6.2 presents the descriptive and readability statistics for the TASA data set as a function of genre and DRP grade level. DRP scores for the passages were highly correlated with both Flesch-Kincaid grade level ($r = .922$) and Flesch Reading Ease ($r = -.925$). Thus, syllables per word, word frequency, words per sentence, and Flesch scores will naturally increase as a function of DRP Grade Level because those variables either contribute to the DRP scores or are highly correlated with variables that contribute to DRP.

These data are presented only to describe the corpus. While all of the comparisons are statistically different in Table 6.2 [virtually all of the $F_{(2,3588)}$ statistics for these comparisons are greater than 100 and all are $p < .001$], some of the comparisons do not provide important information about the texts because of the constraints on this particular corpus. For example, the number of sentences per passage decreases across grade levels because the number of words per sentences increases across grade levels (by definition of grade level) and because the length of passage is controlled; that is, the number of words is controlled in TASA such that the passages are of relatively equal lengths.

Regarding differences between genres, there are two general results of interest that are indicative of the relative difficulty levels of the three genres. First, word difficulty in narrative texts is lower when compared to social stud-

Table 6.2. Descriptive statistics as a function of genre and DRP grade level

	Grade 2						Grade 5					
	Narrative		Social S.		Science		Narrative		Social S.		Science	
	M	SD	M	SD	M	SD	M	SD	M	SD	M	SD
Number of words	280.91	22.04	274.62	21.26	275.51	19.86	281.65	27.59	276.03	21.98	272.85	18.66
Number of sentences	30.19	7.46	30.56	7.02	31.85	6.69	19.93	5.78	22.72	4.18	24.44	4.17
Words per sentences	9.85	2.47	9.36	1.81	8.97	1.73	15.49	5.67	12.52	2.38	11.48	2.09
Flesch-Kincaid Grade	3.14	1.21	3.49	1.15	2.93	1.03	6.19	1.68	6.08	1.11	5.30	1.01
Flesch Reading Ease	89.82	5.53	86.66	6.43	89.92	5.59	77.73	6.23	73.80	6.55	77.51	5.96
Syllables per word	1.26	0.07	1.31	0.07	1.27	0.07	1.34	0.07	1.42	0.08	1.39	0.07
Celex Word Frequency[1]	444.25	716.35	255.22	412.43	175.09	381.68	186.70	403.42	162.37	379.97	94.44	259.02
Content Word Concreteness	398.45	23.822	399.68	23.08	404.43	33.23	396.38	27.836	394.50	27.25	400.29	28.8

	Grade 8						Grade 11					
	Narrative		Social S.		Science		Narrative		Social S.		Science	
	M	SD	M	SD	M	SD	M	SD	M	SD	M	SD
Number of words	285.44	23.22	283.75	24.00	276.43	21.13	292.49	27.11	294.03	23.47	281.23	21.70
Number of sentences	15.25	3.98	18.40	3.71	21.16	3.92	13.43	3.76	16.47	3.35	18.59	3.92
Words per sentences	20.14	6.26	16.17	4.44	13.50	2.68	23.69	8.03	18.69	4.70	15.82	3.73
Flesch-Kincaid Grade	8.67	1.57	8.30	1.13	7.29	0.86	10.61	1.29	10.03	1.12	9.02	1.19
Flesch Reading Ease	67.45	5.65	63.97	5.11	66.84	4.78	56.11	7.36	55.35	5.53	58.26	5.72
Syllables per word	1.41	0.06	1.49	0.07	1.49	0.07	1.50	0.08	1.57	0.08	1.57	0.08
Celex Word Frequency[1]	89.12	345.39	67.31	272.86	50.24	192.22	41.36	226.56	78.75	330.23	53.69	305.88
Content Word Concreteness	389.06	28.97	384.98	27.85	396.19	31.44	380.71	30.50	373.98	388.29	385.21	28.93

ies and science texts. This was found according to both number of syllables
per word ($M_{narrative}$ = 1.37; M_{social} = 1.45; $M_{science}$ = 1.43) and word frequency[1]
($M_{narrative}$ = 190.38; M_{social} = 140.91; $M_{science}$ = 93.36). In contrast, word concreteness indicates that science texts ($M_{science}$ = 396.53) and narrative texts
($M_{narrative}$ = 391.15) contain more concrete words compared to social studies
texts (M_{social} = 388.29). This result regarding the science texts, however, may
be due to rare words in the science text, which may not be available in the
MRC database used to compute word concreteness.

In contrast to word difficulty, sentence-level difficulty decreases monotonically across narrative, social studies, and science texts according to the number of words per sentence ($M_{narrative}$ = 17.19; M_{social} = 14.18; $M_{science}$ = 12.44)
and Flesch-Kincaid grade level ($M_{narrative}$ = 7.15; M_{social} = 6.97; $M_{science}$ = 6.14).
Hence, according to these two indices, narrative texts are more challenging at
the sentence level than are social studies and science texts. However, according to Flesch Reading Ease, social studies texts (M_{social} = 69.95) have lower
reading ease scores than do narrative and science texts ($M_{narrative}$ = 72.78;
$M_{science}$ = 73.13).

Thus, it appears that narrative texts have the least challenging words but
the most challenging sentences. Whereas social studies texts have the most
challenging words, they compensate for this less so than do science texts at
the sentence level; that is, social studies texts may be equally or more challenging than science texts at the sentence level and contain greater challenges
at the lexical level.

COREFERENCE AND LSA

Coreference occurs when a noun, pronoun, or noun phrase refers to another
constituent in the text. Coh-Metrix provides several classes of coreference.
However, analyses indicated that all of the coreference indices were highly
correlated and yielded highly similar results. Therefore, we present only the
results for the indices that are available on the Coh-Metrix Web Tool (v1.4).
These include argument overlap, stem overlap, and LSA, crossed with adjacent and all distances. Adjacent overlap refers to overlap between a sentence
and its preceding sentence. The *all* distances index includes the overlap between each sentence and all other sentences in the text. This is intended as a
more global index of cohesion.

Argument overlap is a measure of when the head nouns (or pronouns) of
noun-phrases overlap between two sentences. The term *argument* is used in
a linguistic sense, with noun/pronoun arguments being contrasted with verb/
adjective predicates (Kintsch & Van Dijk, 1978). Argument overlap occurs

when there is overlap between a noun in one sentence and the same noun (in singular or plural form) in another sentence; it also occurs when there is a matching pronoun between two sentences.

Stem overlap occurs when a noun in one sentence refers to a word in another sentence with the same lemma (i.e., core morphological element, be it a noun, verb, adjective, or adverb). Thus, stem overlap could include overlap between *giver* in one sentence and *giver, giving, gives,* or *gave* in another sentence. Both argument overlap and stem overlap also include overlap between a pronoun in one sentence and the same pronoun in another sentence.

We also show two types of LSA indices: adjacent sentence to sentence, and sentence to all other sentences. LSA is a statistical method to determine semantic relations between words, sentences and paragraphs by using higher-order co-occurrences (Landauer & Dumais, 1997). LSA has been shown to reflect human knowledge in a variety of ways. For example, LSA measures correlate highly with human scores on standard vocabulary and subject matter tests; it mimics human word sorting and category judgments; it simulates word–word and passage–word lexical priming data; it has been used to estimate passage coherence; it grades essays as well as experts in English composition (Landauer et al., 2007).

The results for each of the indices are presented in Figure 6.1 and Tables 6.3, 6.4, and 6.5. As shown in Table 6.3, there were main effects of DRP grade level and genre, and interactions between the two factors for all six referential cohesion indices. As shown in Table 6.4, the main effect of DRP

Table 6.3. F table for cohesion indices

Category	Index	Genre $F(2,3588)$	DRP Grade $F(3,3588)$	Interaction $F(6,3588)$	MSe
Local	Argument Overlap Adj	220.32	72.62	9.20	0.032
Referential	Stem Overlap Adj	218.84	107.19	14.39	0.029
Cohesion	LSA Sent to Sent	683.63	5.16	4.10	0.009
Global	Argument Overlap All	36.13	144.55	7.51	0.025
Referential	Stem Overlap All	35.66	204.29	7.85	0.024
Cohesion	LSA All Sentences	351.21	42.98	1.41 (NS)	0.007
Verb	LSA Verb Cohesion	230.73	274.20	4.98	0.001
Cohesion	WordNet Verb Cohesion	184.76	94.96	1.85 (NS)	0.013
	Causal	25.86	0.78 (NS)	3.16 (p=.004)	89.53
Connectives	Additive	144.38	63.72	2.06 (p=.055)	228.78
Incidence	Temporal	72.79	7.72	4.74	74.96
	Clarification	50.14	36.24	2.37 (p=.028)	2.48
	All Connectives	98.98	45.04	5.25	359.94
Causal Ratio	COS Verbs Incidence	240.02	30.48	2.10 (p=.050)	161.18
Index	Connective to Verb Ratio	11.83	7.81	4.88	0.62

P values all < .001 unless noted; COS Verbs refer to Change-of-State Verbs

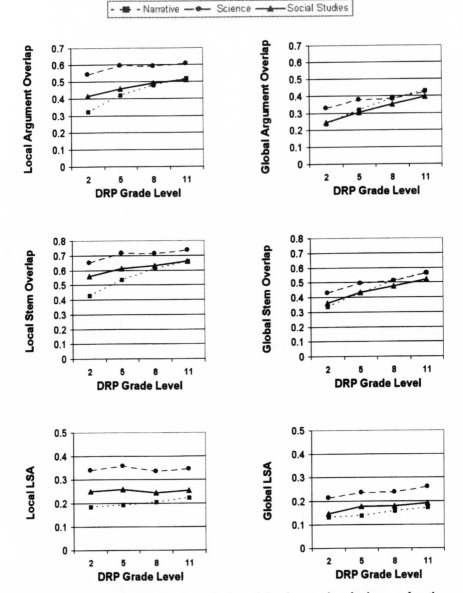

Figure 6.1.   Local and global indices of referential and semantic cohesion as a function of genre and DRP grade level.

Table 6.4. Cohesion indices as a function of DRP grade levels

		DRP Grade Level							
		2.00		5.00		8.00		11.00	
Category	Index	M	SD	M	SD	M	SD	M	SD
Local	Argument Overlap Adj	0.43	0.19	0.49	0.19	0.52	0.19	0.55	0.20
Referential	Stem Overlap Adj	0.55	0.19	0.62	0.19	0.65	0.18	0.68	0.18
Cohesion	LSA Sent to Sent	0.26	0.11	0.27	0.11	0.26	0.11	0.27	0.11
Global	Argument Overlap All	0.27	0.14	0.33	0.16	0.37	0.16	0.42	0.18
Referential	Stem Overlap All	0.38	0.14	0.45	0.16	0.50	0.16	0.55	0.17
Cohesion	LSA All Sentences	0.16	0.08	0.18	0.09	0.19	0.09	0.21	0.10
Verb Cohesion	LSA Verb Cohesion	0.06	0.04	0.05	0.03	0.04	0.02	0.04	0.02
	WordNet Verb Cohesion	0.60	0.13	0.55	0.12	0.52	0.11	0.49	0.11
	Causal	16.40	10.22	16.92	9.79	16.64	9.02	17.01	9.09
Connectives	Additive	38.28	15.56	43.62	16.21	46.84	16.09	46.78	15.02
Incidence	Temporal	13.77	9.61	13.32	9.31	13.11	8.35	11.89	8.06
	Clarification	0.15	0.87	0.50	1.52	0.61	1.66	0.92	2.09
	All Connectives	64.60	21.37	70.94	19.96	73.65	18.93	73.55	17.75
Causal Ratio	COS Verbs Incidence	27.01	14.96	26.44	14.74	24.14	12.29	21.90	11.80
Index	Connective to Verb Ratio	0.72	0.87	0.72	0.71	0.76	0.69	0.88	0.89

Table 6.5. Cohesion Indices as a function of genre

		Genre					
		Narrative		Social Studies		Science	
Category	Index	M	SD	M	SD	M	SD
Local	Argument Overlap Adj	0.44	0.20	0.47	0.18	0.58	0.17
Referential	Stem Overlap Adj	0.56	0.21	0.62	0.18	0.70	0.15
Cohesion	LSA Sent to Sent	0.20	0.09	0.25	0.09	0.34	0.11
Global	Argument Overlap All	0.34	0.18	0.32	0.16	0.38	0.16
Referential	Stem Overlap All	0.46	0.19	0.45	0.16	0.50	0.15
Cohesion	LSA All Sentences	0.15	0.07	0.17	0.08	0.24	0.10
Verb	LSA Verb Cohesion	0.04	0.02	0.04	0.03	0.06	0.03
Cohesion	WordNet Verb Cohesion	0.51	0.12	0.54	0.12	0.57	0.13
Connectives	Causal	15.99	8.42	15.89	9.71	18.35	10.22
	Additive	49.52	16.32	42.98	14.94	39.14	15.29
Incidence	Temporal	15.39	8.73	12.44	8.74	11.24	8.66
	Clarification	0.28	1.15	0.46	1.46	0.90	2.05
	All Connectives	76.96	19.30	68.01	19.61	67.09	19.23
Causal Ratio	COS Verbs Incidence	20.59	10.00	22.72	11.42	31.31	16.30
Index	Connective to Verb Ratio	0.83	0.80	0.79	0.91	0.68	0.65

grade level reflects an increase of cohesion across the grade levels for all six measures.

For the local, adjacent indices, the main effect of genre reflected the finding that narrative had the lowest and science had the highest referential cohesion (see Table 6.5). Figure 6.1 shows that this difference is more accentuated for the DRP grade levels 2 and 5. For DRP grade levels 8 and 11, there are reduced differences between narrative and social studies texts according to the local cohesion indices.

The results for the global (all sentence) indices also show greater cohesion for science texts and lower cohesion for narrative texts (see Table 6.5). However, the global stem overlap index did not show a significant difference between narrative and social studies texts. According to the global argument and stem overlap measures, the narrative texts increase more in cohesion across the grade levels than do the social studies and science texts. Thus, in comparison to the narrative texts, the science texts are more cohesive in the earlier DRP grade levels, but the narrative texts catch up in the later grades. Whereas there is little difference in global cohesion at grade 2 comparing narrative and social studies texts, narrative texts are more cohesive than social studies texts as DRP grade levels increase.

An interaction between genre and DRP grade level was found for the LSA sentence-to-sentence index, but not for the LSA all-sentence index. The interaction between DRP grade and genre for the sentence-to-sentence LSA index reflects the finding that the increase in cohesion across the grades is only significant for the narrative texts, $F(3,1196)=11.08$, and is not significant for either the social studies texts, $F(3,1196)=2.48$, or science texts, $F(3,1196)=1.31$. This is analogous to the larger increase in cohesion across grades observed for the narrative texts according to the argument overlap and stem overlap indices.

Verb Cohesion

The observation of lower referential cohesion in the lower-grade texts sparks the question of what might compensate in texts that are more likely to be read by young children for this marked lack of referential cohesion. One answer to that question is that children's texts tend to have more pictures and those pictures might add some degree of referential cohesion (Carney & Levin, 2002; Fang, 1996).

Because we cannot investigate that possibility in this study (i.e., TASA texts contain no pictures), we pursue an alternative explanation here that texts with lower DRP grade levels might compensate for referential cohesion with verb cohesion (Turner, Britton, Andraessen, & McCutchen, 1996). That is, perhaps there is greater overlap in what is happening, rather than the people and objects that are acting in the sentences. Perhaps actions carry the weight in lower-grade texts, rather than objects.

To test this hypothesis, we developed two new algorithms to measure verb overlap within paragraphs. In each paragraph, we compared all pairs of verbs and calculated the average degree of overlap for each verb pair by two algorithms, namely LSA and WordNet. In the LSA algorithm, the cosine of two LSA vectors corresponding to the given pair of verbs is used to represent the degree of overlap of the two verbs. In the WordNet algorithm, the overlap was a binary representation: 1 when two verbs were in the same synonym set and 0 otherwise. The results from these two indices are presented in Figure 6.2 and Tables 6.3, 6.4, and 6.5. As expected, verb cohesion was greater in the earlier DRP grade texts than in the later grade texts, as reflected by main effects of grade level for both indices. There were significant differences between all grade levels except grades 8 and 11 for the LSA index.

Also, verb cohesion decreases monotonically across science, social studies, and narrative texts, as reflected by main effects of genre and significant differences between all three genres. The interaction of grade level and genre was significant according the LSA index but not the WordNet index. The source of the interaction for the LSA index seemed to be a lack of a difference between narrative and social studies texts at grade 2 compared to reliable differences for grades 5, 8, and 11.

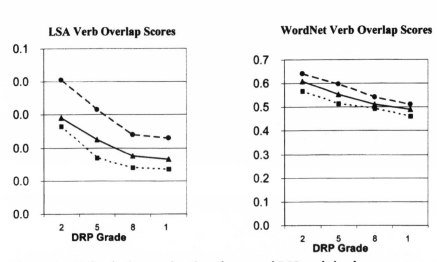

Figure 6.2.   Verb cohesion as a function of genre and DRP grade level.

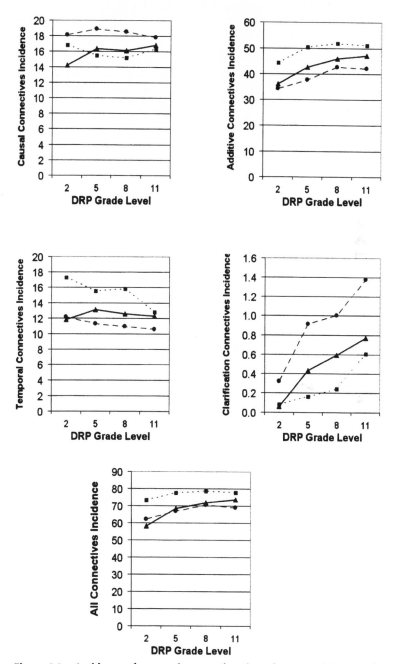

Figure 6.3. Incidence of connectives as a function of genre and DRP grade level.

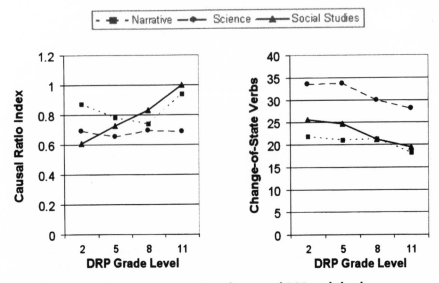

Figure 6.4.   Causal cohesion as a function of genre and DRP grade level.

Connectives

Another element of cohesion in text comes from connectives, such as *therefore, consequently,* and *because.* Connectives provide more explicit cues to the type of relationship between ideas in a text, and thus increase text cohesion (Halliday & Hasan, 1976; Louwerse, 2001). Coh-Metrix provides an incidence score (occurrence per 1,000 words) for four general types of connectives: causal, additive, temporal, and clarification. Coh-Metrix also provides an incidence score for all of these connectives combined.

The results for indices for connectives are presented in Tables 6.3, 6.4, and 6.5, and Figures 6.3 and 6.4. Table 6.3 shows that all five indices for the incidence (number per 1,000 words) of connectives showed main effects of genre; four of the five showed effects of DRP grade level; and the interactions between genre and grade level ranged from marginal to significant for the five indices. Across the indices, science texts had more causal and clarification connectives, whereas narratives had more additive and temporal connectives. Most of the indices either show no change or increase as a function of grade level, though temporal connectives showed a decrease for grade 11 narrative texts. The details for these results follow.

Causal Connectives

Causal connectives cue the reader to make a causal relation between two text segments. Examples of causal connectives include *because, so, a con-*

sequence of, after all, nevertheless, and *although.* The main effect of genre for causal connectives reflects the finding that there were significantly more causal connectives in science texts, with no difference between social studies and narrative texts. This is not a surprise, because causal relations can easily be formed in narrative texts without an explicit causal cue. There were no differences as a function of grade level. As shown in Figure 6.3, the interaction reflects a significant effect of grade level for the social studies texts, $F(3,1196) = 4.22$, $p = .004$, compared to nonsignificant effects for narrative, $F(3,1196) = 2.49$, $p = .059$, and science texts, $F<1$. For social studies texts, there was a rise in causal verbs after grade 2, but no differences between grades 5, 8, and 11.

Additive Connectives

Additive connectives cue the reader that two text segments need to be tied together, as in the case of *also, as well, further, anyhow, moreover,* and *furthermore.* There was a significant increase in additive connectives among science, social studies, and narrative texts. Additive connectives also increased from grades 2 to 8, with no difference between grades 8 and 11. The interaction shown in Figure 6.3 was only marginally significant.

Temporal Connectives

Temporal connectives cue the reader to make a temporal relation between segments. Examples of temporal connectives are *before, after, up to now, until then,* and *while.* There was a significant monotonic increase in temporal connectives between science, social studies, and narrative texts. For the effect of grade level, there was no change from grades 2 to 8 and significant decrease for grade 11 texts. The interaction shown in Figure 6.3 indicates that this decrease for grade 11 texts only occurred for the narrative texts, $F(3,1196) = 14.47$, $p<.001$, but not for the social studies and science texts (both $F<2$).

Clarification Connectives

Clarification connectives cue the reader that the writer is restating previous text in different words or providing examples to illustrate a concept. Examples of clarification connectives include *that is to say, in other words,* and *for example.* There were very few clarification connectives in the texts. Nonetheless, there was an increase among narrative, social studies, and science texts. There was a general increase across the grade levels, with no difference between grades 5 and 8. Thus, the texts estimated at grade level 11 by the DRP scores contained approximately one clarification connective per 1,000 words.

There was also an interaction between genre and grade level (see Figure 6.3) indicating that this increase varied by genre. Science and social studies texts showed the same general pattern, with no differences between grades 5 and 8 or between grades 8 and 11. In contrast, narratives show a significant increase only for grade 11 texts, and no difference between grade levels 2, 5, and 8.

All Connectives

The overall number of connectives indicate that there were more connectives overall in the narrative texts, with no difference between the science and social studies texts. This effect is evidently carried by the greater number of additive connectives. There was a general increase in connectives from grade 2 to 11, with significant differences between grades 2, 5 and 8, but no difference between grades 8 and 11. There was also an interaction (see Figure 6.3) indicating that this pattern occurred only for the social studies texts. In contrast, for narratives and science texts, the difference in grade levels was significant only between grade level 2 and the other grade levels; no differences between grades 5, 8, and 11 were observed.

Causal Ratio Index

Coh-Metrix also provides an index of causal cohesion by measuring the ratio of the incidence of causal connectives to *change-of-state* (COS) verbs (i.e., causal connectives/(COS verbs+1). COS verbs are those verbs that refer to changes of state (*break, freeze*), actions (*impact, hit)*, or events (*move*) rather than states (according to WordNet).

A text is judged as more causally cohesive to the extent that there are more causal connectives that relate actions and events in the text. If there are numerous action and event verbs without causal connectives to aid the reader, then the reader is more likely to be forced to generate inferences to understand the relationships between the actions and events in the sentences. We examined the incidence of COS verbs and the ratio of the incidence of causal connectives to COS verbs (i.e., causal connectives/(COS verbs+1); a text is considered more causally cohesive to the extent that there are more causal connectives that relate the actions and events in the text.

There were more COS verbs in science texts, and in turn, more in social studies, than in narrative texts. There was also a decrease in the incidence of COS verbs going from grades 2 to 11, although the difference between grades 2 and 5 was not significant. As shown in Figure 6.4, this decrease across the grade levels depended on genre. For narratives, the differences between grades 2, 5, and 8 were not significant. In contrast, for science and social studies texts the differences appeared comparing grades 2 and 5 to grades 8 and 11.

The ratio index reveals the critical relationship between causal connectives and COS verbs. Because the number of causal connectives did not compensate for the greater number of change-of-state verbs, the ratio was lowest for science texts as compared to social studies and narrative texts, which were not significantly different. There was an effect of grade level reflecting a difference between the grade levels 2, 5, and 8 as compared to grade 11. However, Figure 6.4 shows that this pattern only occurred for the narrative texts, $F(3,1196) = 3.92$, $p = .008$. There was no change across the grades for the science texts, $F<1$, compared to a monotonic increase for social studies texts, $F(3,1196) = 10.34$, $p<.001$.

CONCLUSION

This corpus study was conducted for the purposes of examining differences in cohesion between text genres associated with different levels of text difficulty and examining differences in text cohesion as a function of grade level of the intended audience for a text. The overarching goal is to provide a better understanding of the characteristics of text as they vary across genres and grade levels. We regard this as a first step toward creating reading assessments for which the nature of the passages is more fully understood.

The analyses of the TASA data allow us to examine text difficulty in two ways. The first follows the general assumption that narrative texts tend to be less challenging to understand than expository texts. The second is that text difficulty is, at least to some degree, related to increases in sentence complexity (sentence length) and word difficulty (word frequency) and thus is related to increases across grades. Thus, our principal goal was to examine how cohesion varied as a function of these two factors: genre and DRP grade level.

DRP grade level is a traditional readability measure and thus correlates highly with the length of the sentence and word frequency. Hence, we are by consequence examining how cohesion varies as a function of readability scores. There is an underlying assumption, nevertheless, that the lower DRP grade level texts would be more likely to be found in lower grade level books, and vice versa, the higher DRP levels would be more likely found in high grade level books.

One question regards the challenges of the texts at the word and sentence levels. The descriptive results in Table 6.2 indicate that in comparison to social studies and science texts, narrative texts have the least challenging words, but the most challenging sentences. In contrast, social studies texts have the most challenging words, but they are also challenging at the sentence level. Thus, they compensate at the sentence level for lexical challenges less so than do science texts.

The results further indicated that there was an increase in referential cohesion across grade levels. Higher-grade-level texts, which are by consequence more difficult at the word and sentence levels, exhibited higher cohesion than lower grade level texts. We also saw that science texts showed the highest cohesion levels. Narrative texts were the least cohesive, but also increased in cohesion across grade levels more than the other two genres.

Thus, in contrast to previous observations that referential cohesion is greater for texts that are better understood (i.e., high cohesion texts; McNamara, O'Reilly, Best, & Ozuru, 2006), we observed here that referential cohesion was lower for texts assumed to be less difficult (i.e., narrative texts and lower grade level texts). Both results follow from the constraints of the texts.

In studies where cohesion is manipulated, high cohesion texts are intended to have higher referential cohesion. In contrast, lower-grade texts examined here have, by definition, shorter sentences, and shorter sentences tend to have lower referential cohesion. Narrative texts have lower referential cohesion because they tend to include more topics, are less challenging at the lexical level (have lower frequency words), and writers tend to "try to use different words" across sentences.

While lower-grade texts lacked referential cohesion, they were higher in verb cohesion. Our supposition was that lower-grade texts may have greater overlap in the actions than in the objects. An extreme example along those lines is a typical text for a very young reader such as: *Mice eat cheese. Cows eat hay. Chickens eat grain.* There is little referential overlap, but perfect verb overlap. Here we saw that verb cohesion was greater in the earlier DRP grade texts than in the later grade texts. Thus, the results here suggest that the lower referential cohesion in the lower grade level texts is in some part compensated for by greater verb cohesion, shorter sentences, and more frequent words.

Connectives are another signature of text cohesion. The results here indicated that the use of connectives tends to increase across the grade levels. Narrative texts tended to have more connectives, particularly additive and temporal connectives. In contrast, science texts tended to have more causal connectives and clarification connectives. While science text contained more causal connectives, they were apparently not sufficient to compensate for the greater number of change-of-state verbs. There were more change-of-state verbs than there were causal connectives to indicate the direction of causality. Thus, the ratio of causal connectives to change-of-state verbs indicated that science texts were the least cohesive.

Table 6.6. **Summary of results in terms of the five sources of text difficulty found for each of the three text genres. High/Medium/Low is used to refer to the degree to which that genre showed greater difficulty in comparison to the other two genres**

	Challenges/Difficulty				
	Word Level	Sentence Level	Referential Cohesion	Verb Cohesion	Connectives
Narratives	Low	High	High	High	Low
Social Studies	High	High/Med	High	Moderate	Moderate
Science	High	Low	Low	Low	High

The results of this study are summarized in Table 6.6, which presents the results in terms of the five sources of text difficulty found for each of the three text genres. High/Medium/Low is used to refer to the degree to which each genre showed greater difficulty in comparison to the other two genres. For example, the narrative texts showed higher word frequency and thus lower challenges at the word level, but lower cohesion, and thus higher challenges at the referential cohesion level.

We can think about the results summarized in this table in terms of prior research on the relative difficulties of narrative compared to expository text, wherein narrative is generally judged as less challenging. As such, it appears from these results comparing the features of these three genres that the source of ease in reading narratives primarily comes from familiarity with the words, as well as the use of connectives. Overall, it seems that the words carry the day.

Conversely, this result corresponds to work in individual differences that show that prior domain and world knowledge are important predictors of how well readers understand expository text. That is, when readers have more knowledge, they are more likely to be familiar with infrequent concepts in expository texts, and thus the frequency of words will have a lesser effect on comprehension performance. In turn, low-knowledge readers will show an exaggerated effect of genre on comprehension, and high-knowledge readers may be expected to show lesser differences in comprehension comparing narrative and expository texts.

Comparing the science and narrative texts, we see that the results are reversed. For the science texts, it appears that two sources of difficulty arise at the word level and from too few connectives. This first result is to be expected: Science texts contain less frequent words. The second seems to stem from a lower ratio of causal connectives to change-of-state verbs as well as a lower number of connectives overall. The concepts are generally less familiar and more abstract, there are numerous change-of-state verbs, and there are too few connectives to communicate the relationships that connect the actions and events in the texts. On the whole, the results indicate that the causality thought to be intrinsic to science texts is not supported well by connectives, which are generally used to indicate the nature of the relationships in the texts.

We additionally found that the science texts displayed relatively high cohesion. There is a general sense that science texts are challenging texts, and substantially more difficult than narratives. However, here we see that science texts have higher referential and verb cohesion in comparison to narrative and social studies texts. This seems to contradict prior research showing the benefits of increased cohesion for science texts (e.g., McNamara et al., 1996).

If we combine results showing that increased cohesion benefits science text comprehension, and these results showing that the cohesion of science texts is relatively high, one implication is that writers do tend to negotiate difficulty by increasing cohesion, but they may not do so quite enough. The cohesion apparent in science texts may not adequately compensate for the increased challenges that arise at conceptual levels.

One question pervading the literature regards the nature of and differences between text genres. We saw here that the narrative/expository distinction in genres is not sufficiently discriminating. Narratives are clearly distinct in many ways from science texts. On the other hand, social studies texts are like narratives in some ways and in other ways like science texts. Unfortunately, it seems that social studies texts have the worst of both worlds.

They appear to have the conceptual difficulty of science texts, but there is little to compensate at other levels. They tend to have long sentences, low cohesion, and a moderate number of connectives. It seems that writers of social studies must assume that readers already have the necessary knowledge to make inferences about events in the world. Indeed, it seems natural to assume that readers will know about many world concepts such as geography, government, civilization, war, and so on.

When the reader does have the necessary knowledge, we can expect these types of texts to be relatively comprehensible. That is, the reader's deeper knowledge of social concepts and the world will help to compensate for cohesion gaps in the texts as well as other linguistic challenges. But when the reader does not have this knowledge, there is little, it seems, in social studies texts to compensate for the challenges.

One way of considering optimal features of text is as a negotiation between different aspects of text difficulty. These results collectively point to tradeoffs between difficulty at the lexical, sentence, and cohesion levels. Such a result suggests that it is insufficient to define readability simply on the basis of word frequency, word length, and sentence length. Text difficulty is also a result of cohesion. The results indicate that writers may engage in a negotiation between features that contribute to text difficulty. When cohesion is low, readability tends to be easier. When readability is more difficult, then word concreteness may be higher. Or, when referential frequency is low, verb cohesion may lend a hand. Essentially, rare should be the text that is *difficult* according to all features of text difficulty, but also rare is the text that is *easy* on all features of text difficulty.

Of course the nature of passages will differ depending on the targeted populations. These analyses do not provide prescriptive data, or optimal text features. They simply provide a better idea of what texts will generally look like. Without such a picture, we can imagine that test developers may attempt to include passages that adhere to only one dimension of text difficulty.

Coh-Metrix indices also offer a potential means for assessing the strengths and weaknesses of readers. By considering the challenges of a text and the performance of the reader, deductions can potentially be drawn concerning the particular strengths and weaknesses of a reader. For example, suppose an assessment were devised that included both high and low cohesion, narrative and science texts. If the reader performed well on the narrative but not the science texts, one might deduce that the reader is low in science domain knowledge and that the reader is unable to compensate for knowledge deficits strategically (e.g., O'Reilly & McNamara, 2007). If the reader performed well on high-cohesion but not low-cohesion texts, an instructor might want to focus on providing the reader with strategies to generate local and global inferences in low cohesion text (e.g., McNamara, 2004).

More hypothetical examples are possible of course. The main point is that understanding text characteristics, in concert with understanding the nature of the types of questions (e.g., McNamara et al., 1996), offers a means to better understand a reader's pedagogical needs.

Our overarching supposition is that test developers should heed multiple dimensions of text difficulty, considering word, sentence, and semantic challenges. More particularly, we propose that cohesion should be considered in concert with other measures of text difficulty. Most importantly, greater cohesion in text alleviates knowledge demands in text. High cohesion is not always necessary, but it is likely to play a critical role in the context of passages composed of challenging words and sentences. Having better and more precise measures of text difficulty (rather than merely length and frequency) will allow us to identify the meaningful and actionable sources of the difficulty and design items and tasks accordingly.

REFERENCES

Baayen, R. H., Piepenbrock, R., & van Rijn, H. (Eds.) (1993). *The CELEX Lexical Database* (CD-ROM). Philadelphia: Linguistic Data Consortium, University of Pennsylvania.

Brill, E. (1992). A simple rule-based part of speech tagger. In *Proceedings of the Third Conference on Applied Natural Language Processing* (pp. 152–55). Strouds-burg, PA: Association for Computational Linguistics.

Britton, B. K., & Gulgoz, S. (1991) Using Kintsch's computational model to improve instructional text: Effects of repairing inference calls on recall and cognitive struc-tures. *Journal of Educational Psychology, 83,* 329–45.

Bruner, J. (1986). *Actual minds, possible worlds.* Cambridge, MA: Harvard Univer-sity Press.

Carney, R., & Levin, J. (2002). Pictorial illustrations *still* improve students' learning from text. *Educational Psychology Review, 14,* 5–26.

Charniak, E. (2000). A maximum-entropy-inspired parser. In *Proceedings of the First Conference on North American Chapter of the Association for Computational Lin-guistics* (pp. 132–39). San Francisco: Morgan Kaufmann Publishers.

Coltheart, M. (1981). The MRC psycholinguistic database quarterly. *Journal of Ex-perimental Psychology, 33A,* 497–505.

Fang, Z. (1996). Illustration, text, and the child reader: What are pictures in children's storybooks for? *Reading Horizons, 37,* 130–42.

Flesch, R. (1948). A new readability yardstick. *Journal of Applied Psychology, 32,* 221–33.

Gernsbacher, M. A. (1990). *Language comprehension as structure building.* Hills-dale, NJ: Lawrence Erlbaum Associates.

Givón, T. 1995. *Functionalism and grammar.* Philadelphia: John Benjamins.

Graesser, A. C., Gernsbacher, M. A., & Goldman, S. (Eds.). (2003). *Handbook of discourse processes.* Mahwah, NJ: Lawrence Erlbaum Associates.

Graesser, A. C., Hauft-Smith, K., Cohen, A. D., & Pyles, L. D. (1980). Advanced outlines, familiarity, text genre, and retention of prose. *Journal of Experimental Education, 48,* 209–20.

Graesser, A. C., Hoffman, N. L., & Clark, L. F. (1980). Structural components of reading time. *Journal of Verbal Learning and Verbal Behavior, 19,* 131–51.

Graesser, A. C., McNamara, D. S., & Louwerse, M. M. (2003). What do readers need to learn in order to process coherence relations in narrative and expository text. In A.P. Sweet and C.E. Snow (Eds.), *Rethinking reading comprehension* (pp. 82–98). New York: Guilford Publications.

Graesser, A. C., McNamara, D. S., Louwerse, M. M., & Cai, Z. (2004). Coh-Metrix: Analysis of text on cohesion and language. *Behavior Research Methods, Instru-ments, and Computers,* 36, 193–202.

Haberlandt, K., & Graesser, A. C. (1985). Component processes in text comprehen-sion and some of their interactions. *Journal of Experimental Psychology: General, 114,* 357–74.

Hall, C., McCarthy, P. M., Lewis, G. A., Lee, D. S., & McNamara, D. S. (2007). A Coh-Metrix assessment of American and English/Welsh Legal English. Coyote papers: Psycholinguistic and computational perspectives. *University of Arizona Working Papers in Linguistics, 15,* 40–54.

Halliday, M. A. K., & Hasan, R. (1976). *Cohesion in English.* London: Longman.

Kintsch, W. (1998). *Comprehension: A paradigm for cognition.* Cambridge: Cambridge University Press.

Kintsch, W., & Van Dijk, T. A. (1978). Toward a model of text comprehension and production. *Psychological Review, 85,* 363–94.

Klare, G. R. (1974–1975). Assessing readability. *Reading Research Quarterly, 10,* 62–102.

Koslin, B.L., Zeno, S., & Koslin, S. (1987). *The DRP: An effective measure in reading.* New York: College Entrance Examination Board.

Landauer, T. K., & Dumais, S. T. (1997). A solution to Plato's problem: The Latent Semantic Analysis theory of the acquisition, induction, and representation of knowledge. *Psychological Review, 104,* 211–240.

Landauer, T., McNamara, D., Dennis, S., & Kintsch, W. (Eds.). (2007) *Handbook of Latent Semantic Analysis.* Mahwah, NJ: Lawrence Erlbaum Associates.

Louwerse, M. (2001). An analytic and cognitive parameterization of coherence relations. *Cognitive Linguistics, 12,* 291–315.

Louwerse, M., McCarthy, P. M., McNamara, D. S., & Graesser, A. C. (2004). Variation in language and cohesion across written and spoken registers. In K. Forbus, D. Gentner, & T. Regier (Eds.), *Proceedings of the 26th Annual Meeting of the Cognitive Science Society* (pp. 843–48). Austin, TX: Cognitive Science Society.

Magliano, J. P., Millis, K. K., Ozuru, Y., & McNamara, D.S. (2007). A multidimensional framework to evaluate reading assessment tools. In D. S. McNamara (Ed.), *Reading comprehension strategies: Theories, interventions, and technologies* (pp. 107–36). Mahwah, NJ: Lawrence Erlbaum Associates.

McCarthy, P. M., Briner, S. W., Rus, V., & McNamara, D. S. (2007). Textual signatures: Identifying text-types using Latent Semantic Analysis to measure the cohesion of text structures. In A. Kao, & S. Poteet (Eds.), *Natural language processing and text mining* (pp. 107–22). London: Springer-Verlag UK.

McCarthy, P. M., Lewis, G. A., Dufty, D. F., & McNamara, D. S. (2006). Analyzing writing styles with Coh-Metrix. In *Proceedings of the Florida Artificial Intelligence Research Society International Conference* (pp. 764–70). Menlo Park, CA: AAAI Press.

McCarthy, P. M., Lightman, E. J., Dufty, D. F., & McNamara, D. S. (2006, July). *Using Coh-Metrix to assess distributions of cohesion and difficulty: An investigation of the structure of high-school textbooks.* Member poster presented at the 28th Annual Conference of the Cognitive Science Society, Vancouver, Canada.

McNamara, D. S. (2001). Reading both high and low coherence texts: Effects of text sequence and prior knowledge. *Canadian Journal of Experimental Psychology, 55,* 51–62.

———. (2004). SERT: Self-explanation reading training. *Discourse Processes, 38,* 1–30.

McNamara, D. S., Kintsch, E., Songer, N. B., & Kintsch, W. (1996). Are good texts always better? Text coherence, background knowledge, and levels of understanding in learning from text. *Cognition and Instruction, 14,* 1–43.

McNamara, D. S., & Kintsch, W. (1996). Learning from text: Effects of prior knowledge and text coherence. *Discourse Processes, 22,* 247–87.

McNamara, D. S., O'Reilly, T., Best, R. & Ozuru, Y. (2006). Improving adolescent students' reading comprehension with iSTART. *Journal of Educational Computing Research, 34*, 147–71.

Miller, G. A, Beckwith, R., Fellbaum, C., Gross, D. & Miller, K. (1990). *Five papers on WordNet.* Cognitive Science Laboratory, Princeton University, No. 43.

O'Reilly, T., & McNamara, D. S. (2007). Reversing the reverse cohesion effect: good texts can be better for strategic, high-knowledge readers. *Discourse Processes, 43*, 121–52.

Rubin, D. C. (1995). *Memory in oral traditions: The cognitive psychology of epic ballads and counting-out rhymes.* New York: Oxford University Press.

Sekine S., & Grishman R. (1995). *A corpus-based probabilistic grammar with only two non-terminals.* In the Fourth International Workshop on Parsing Technology. Prague, Czech Republic.

Stenner, A. J. (1996). *Measuring reading comprehension with the Lexile Framework.* Durham, NC: MetaMetrics, Inc.

Tonjes, M.J., Wolpow, R., & Zintz, M.V. (1999). *Integrated content literacy.* New York: The McGraw-Hill Publishers.

Turner, A., Britton, B. K., Andraessen, P. B., & McCutchen, D. (1996). A predication semantics model of text comprehension and recall. In B.K. Britton and A.C. Graesser (Eds*), Models of text understanding* (pp. 33–72). Mahwah, NJ: Lawrence Erlbaum Associates.

VanderVeen, A., Huff, K., Gierl, M., McNamara, D. S., Louwerse, M., & Graesser, A.C. (2007). Developing and validating instructionally relevant reading competency profiles measured by the critical reading sections of the SAT. In D.S. McNamara (Ed.), *Reading comprehension strategies: Theories, interventions, and technologies* (pp. 137–72). Mahwah, NJ: Lawrence Erlbaum Associates.

Zwaan, R. A., & Radvansky, G. A. (1998). Situation models in language comprehension and memory. *Psychological Bulletin, 123*, 162–85.

NOTE

1. Word frequency is measured by the Celex index of word frequency for the lowest frequency content word per sentence (Baayen, Piepenbrock, & van Rijn, 1993). The underlying assumption of this measure is that sentence comprehension is most constrained by the rarest words in a sentence. We used the raw measure here because it is more interpretable than the logarithm transformation. However, it is notably skewed. Thus, we advise that the logarithm transformation should be used for most statistical analyses that focus on word frequency.

Section II

THE SCIENCE OF ASSESSMENT
AND THE PROFICIENT READER

Chapter Seven

How Research on Reading and Research on Assessment Are Transforming Reading Assessment (or if They Aren't, How They Ought To)

Robert J. Mislevy & John P. Sabatini

INTRODUCTION

Building on developments in the cognitive sciences, contemporary research is providing new insights into the nature and acquisition of reading. We are coming to understand the processes and knowledge that come into play, how they interact, and how they interact differently for readers at different development levels, or even the same reader in different literacy situations (e.g., McNamara, 2007; Vellutino et al., 1996). We are recognizing different etiologies among struggling readers (e.g., Fletcher, Coulter, & Reschly, 2004; Fletcher, Denton, & Francis, 2005; Wayman, Wallace, Wiley, Ticha, & Espin, 2007; Vellutino, Fletcher, Snowling, & Scanlon, 2004) and seeing how compensation strategies can mask difficulties that manifest themselves only under special circumstances (e.g., Walczyk, Marsiglia, Johns, & Bryan, 2004).

At the same time, we are becoming acutely aware of the limitations of familiar practices used in the testing of reading, both for diagnosing individual students and for characterizing populations in large-scale assessments that are meant to support educational policy. Fundamental rethinking of reading assessment is in order.

This chapter describes a significant change that has emerged in educational assessment since the 1990s, namely the view of assessment as evidentiary argument, and looks toward its implications for building and using reading assessments that reflect contemporary reading research. Key strands in reading research are noted, along with implications for assessment practice. The ideas are illustrated with examples from current projects.

DEVELOPMENTS IN ASSESSMENT

A Turning Point

Since the early 1900s, the principal frame for educational and psychological testing has been that of measurement. It has proved invaluable for organizing practical work, including guiding test construction, gauging accuracy, and supporting practical testing applications. But the processes by which examinees produce responses, the nature of the knowledge and capabilities that enable their performances, and the connection between task features and cognitive requirements all lay outside the measurement metaphor.

The third edition of *Educational Measurement* (Linn, 1989) marked a turning point in two ways that are central to this chapter. Messick's (1989) landmark chapter on validity introduces Toulmin's (1958) general structure for arguments as a tool for designing and drawing inferences from assessments. Snow and Lohman's (1989) chapter on cognitive psychology proposes a radical rethinking of the psychological foundations of assessments. Snow and Lohman assert that:

> Summary test scores, and factors based on them, have often been thought of as "signs" indicating the presence of underlying, latent traits. . . . An alternative interpretation of test scores as samples of cognitive processes and contents, and of correlations as indicating the similarity or overlap of this sampling, is equally justifiable and could be theoretically more useful. The evidence from cognitive psychology suggests that test performances are comprised of complex assemblies of component information-processing actions that are adapted to task requirements during performance. The implication is that sign-trait interpretations of test scores and their intercorrelations are superficial summaries at best. At worst, they have misled scientists, and the public, into thinking of fundamental, fixed entities, measured in amounts. Whatever their practical value as summaries, for selection, classification, certification, or program evaluation, the cognitive psychological view is that such interpretations no longer suffice as scientific explanations of aptitude and achievement constructs (p. 317).

The significance of this stance for our purposes is this: A global "reading proficiency" construct may be useful in broad indicators for monitoring system policies or students' progress, but it is not adequate for designing an assessment or fully understanding the information an assessment provides. Constructing more focused assessments and properly interpreting standard reading comprehension scores both require working from a more contemporary understanding of reading—a sociocognitive perspective (Atkinson, 2002) that draws on results on learning and comprehension *within* individuals (e.g., Kintsch, 1998; Hawkins & Blakeslee, 2004) as well as research on shared patterns of meaning and interaction *between* individuals (e.g., Gee, 1992; Strauss & Quinn, 1998).

Assessment as Argument

The argument framework for assessment provides tools to tackle this challenge. The key is that the roles of psychological perspectives, evaluation procedures, and task features—all absent from the measurement framework—are now explicit in assessment argument structures, to be articulated with measurement machinery. Subsequent to Messick's chapter, Kane (1992, 2006) fleshed out and detailed the steps in validity arguments and Bachman (2005) extended the framework to assessment use arguments. Mislevy and his colleagues (Mislevy & Haertel, 2006; Mislevy, Steinberg, & Almond, 2003) built further on this foundation to explicate the connections among assessment arguments, task design, evaluation methods, and measurement models in a research program called evidence-centered assessment design (ECD).

Figure 7.1 depicts an assessment design argument in the lower dashed rectangle and an associated assessment use argument in the upper rectangle. Assessment *claims* are shown in the center of the figure. They are both the *outcome* of the assessment design argument and the *data* for the assessment use argument. The terms in which claims are cast connect our thinking about what we observe in the assessment setting with a purpose such as evaluating policy or guiding students' learning. We ground a claim with *data*. At the bottom of the figure is a student's action in a situation: the students says, does, or makes something. Interpretations of these actions are data in an assessment argument, but they are not the only data. Equally important are aspects of the situation in which the student is acting and other information about the student's relationship to the observational situation that may be important in interpreting the action.

The "assessment as argument" perspective holds important implications for the design and use of reading assessments. Note that Figure 7.1 focuses on the structure and the substance of the argument. The measurement model comes later, as quantitative machinery to work with evidence and uncertainty, just one portion of the reasoning carried out in a predominantly qualitative argument (Mislevy, 2006, 2009).

One conceives students' capabilities in a way that suits the intended use of the assessment. These capabilities are represented in the figure as the claim and operationalized as scores in measurement models. What they actually mean is shaped by this intention: the design choices about texts and task settings; what activity will be observed and how it will be evaluated; and

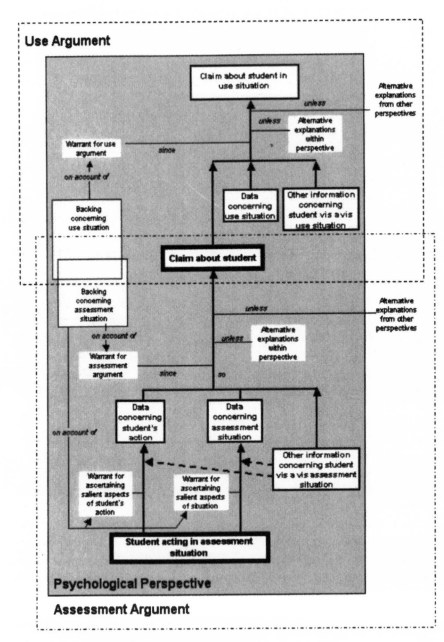

Use Argument

Claim about student in use situation

Alternative explanations from other perspectives

unless

unless Alternative explanations within perspective

Warrant for use argument

since

on account of

Backing concerning use situation

Data concerning use situation

Other information concerning student vis a vis use situation

Claim about student

Backing concerning assessment situation

Alternative explanations from other perspectives

unless

on account of

Warrant for assessment argument

unless Alternative explanations within perspective

since

so

Data concerning student's action

Data concerning assessment situation

Other information concerning student vis a vis assessment situation

on account of

Warrant for ascertaining salient aspects of student's action

Warrant for ascertaining salient aspects of situation

Student acting in assessment situation

Psychological Perspective

Assessment Argument

Figure 7.1. Structure for assessment arguments.

the range and variety of tasks that comprise the assessment. The necessary coordination of purpose, task design, and measurement model clarifies why scores from a standard reading comprehension test might provide adequate indicators for a school or a district, but we need diagnostic tests that look quite different on the surface to help struggling students (Rayner, Foorman, Perfetti, Pesetsky, & Seidenberg, 2001; Sabatini, 2009).

Integrating Cognition, Design, and Analysis

Being able to build assessments that evoke targeted mixtures of capabilities requires being able to create tasks with predictable demands with respect to targeted aspects of knowledge. A distinct line of assessment research that dovetails with the argument framework does exactly this. ECD, for example, builds on foundational work integrating cognitive research, task design, and measurement modeling, such as Embretson (1985, 1998) and Tatsuoka (1983).

Much of this work currently falls under the heading of cognitive diagnosis modeling (e.g., Leighton & Gierl, 2007; Rupp, this volume). Gorin and Embretson (2006) show how the ideas are applied in the domain of reading. This finer degree of control of task features in light of cognitive theory proves useful for improving practice in both large-scale assessments of broad proficiency, such as reading comprehension tests, and for the more targeted assessments needed for individual diagnosis or experimental work in reading research.

DEVELOPMENTS IN THE SCIENCE OF READING

Consistent with Snow and Lohman's assertion, research across such fields as psychology, neuroscience, anthropology, and linguistics highlights "the intricate complexity of the unique moment in which a person interacts with an unprecedented material, social and cultural setting" (Claxton, 2001). Many things happen at once, at many levels, and much that is important is not conscious. Important advances in reading research can be seen through this lens.

We can distinguish developments at three distinguishable levels that hold importance for the design and use of reading assessments. At the most detailed grain size, focusing mainly on information-processing within persons, the concerns are such issues as the alphabetic principle, oral language development, and orthography. Decoding is primary, then assembling words, phrases, and sentences. A somewhat arbitrary dividing line can be drawn as an upper limit to this level, where a reader constructs the surface meanings of propositions expressed by sentences, or what W. Kintsch (1998) calls a textbase.

A second level concerns the integration of this information with the knowledge the reader brings to the setting, including knowledge of the world, the constructions and genres used, and the reader's and writer's purposes to produce what W. Kintsch (1998) calls a situation model. Traditional reading comprehension tests contain some mix of tasks that require reasoning from a textbase, then constructing and, ultimately, reasoning from a situation model (E. Kintsch, 2005).

A third level, reflecting a sociocultural perspective, concerns the forms, purposes, contexts, and uses of reading that are important in communities. Considerations at this level help us think through the kinds of texts, tasks, and contexts that we might expect of basic or proficient readers at fourth grade, a generally proficient adult, or a specialist in some domain or profession.

Different purposes of assessment reflect qualitatively different assessment arguments and can entail sometimes strikingly different assessment strategies to support them. Attention may focus at different levels among the three listed above.

CRITICAL ASSESSMENTS AND ASSESSMENT ARGUMENTS

This section offers snippets of assessment arguments and use scenarios derived from the science of reading as applied to present-day problems faced by our education system in producing a proficient reading citizenry. We begin with a brief discussion of comprehension level outcomes testing. The focus here is on a select set of construct coverage and developmental issues. We then discuss the nature of surface-level efficient processing of text. The example is of a screening diagnostic assessment approach.

Assessment Arguments for State and other Outcome Comprehension Tests

We begin with a claim about what students *ought* to be able to do. We believe that students ought to read and comprehend at a proficiency level that is adequate to pass an annual state level reading achievement test or comparable off-the-shelf comprehension assessment. This is a relatively narrow and somewhat nontheoretical claim about reading proficiency, defined with respect to the social values and demands of the educational system.

Its intersection with cognitive and related science is in the judgment that the nature of such tests is within the more robust, generalized proficiency ability of a skilled reader. That is, skilled readers of any kind should find it relatively easy to bring their skills to bear in this type of test setting, given adequate preparation (a smattering of test preparation about the type of tasks and setting requirements). Some subset of the knowledge and skills necessary will be relatively specific to specific curriculum standards of a state, but by and large, a good reader should be able to travel across state lines and remain proficient, as measured on such tests. To forward our argument, we will take as a given that state tests pass this minimal threshold of validity (though with some caveats below).

Given how typical off-the-shelf and state tests are structured, what we infer from a student getting a proficient score is as follows. Students are deemed proficient readers because they are able to read texts at their grade level (with respect to expected vocabulary, sentence structure, rhetorical structures, and topical content) and answer questions of those texts that require literal under-standing of the text presented; inferences connecting information within the text itself; inferences demonstrating use of common background knowledge (unless they did not have that background knowledge, or their background knowledge itself was sufficient to answer the question without reference to the target text); and understanding of some range of rhetorical structures of texts and how those influence the meaning and purpose of different texts.

Throughout this volume are discussions of how these outcome tests could be improved with respect to construct coverage and instructional utility, and better convergence with current science and theory.

Note in this description that most of the knowledge and processes at the first level—from decoding up through surface comprehension—are not analyzed in any detail; the central claim is about whether students can marshal them to carry out the kinds of tasks set out in these tests, using the kinds of texts in the kinds of situations presented. It is a claim about what satisfactory performance looks like in these terms at a given grade level. A successful student can be presumed to have the necessary capabilities at adequate levels, and coordinate them sufficiently well, to carry out the tasks that characterize the claim. Little more can be said about students who do not perform at the targeted levels.

With a claim defined in this way, meaning arises from design choices about: (1) the kinds of texts to include, (2) the kinds of tasks, and (3) the conditions of assessment. And in standard reading comprehension tests, the standard choices are, respectively: (1) a socially valued but decidedly constrained set of genres and topics, increasing in complexity over grades, (2) tasks that are mostly inferences limited to the textbase, though at higher grades with more concerning situation models and contextualization, and (3) texts and tasks that are not specifically connected with students' learning his-tory, interests, or goals.

Our point is not that these features do not necessarily make such a test invalid or unuseful, because it can be quite useful for the intended purpose. The point is that we can now see the test not as a measure of a well-defined human ability of reading comprehension, but rather a circumscribed collection of observation opportunities, from a universe of many that could be defined, that highlight a certain configuration of the manifest of knowledge and skills we now know people draw on to construct meaning from texts in different circumstances.

Different collections of tasks, highlighting different configurations of knowledge and skill, could be assembled for different purposes or under different sets of constraints. We bear the responsibility to explain how the design decisions serve the intended purpose; assessment design and assessment use arguments provide a framework for doing so.

School systems are now required to take a summative snapshot of individuals' reading proficiency at least once per year for most of their school careers, though many are adding benchmark tests quarterly to better monitor reading progress (or to predict performance on state tests later in year). This situation poses the developmental question: What cognitive skills are developing, changing and growing across these spans?

The "bookends" of this question—kindergarten and generally proficient adult readers—can somewhat be identified, at least with respect to the text (as opposed to task) side of this equation. A kindergartener or first grader reads printed texts with simple words and grammatical structures. Complexity intrudes even here, as five- and six-year-olds already have well-developed language skills used for oral comprehension and reasoning that typically exceed the demands put upon them in responding to the primitive printed texts they are given.

Assessments designed purely based on printed texts that young children can read may underestimate the variability in comprehension at the earliest grade levels, and would be usefully supplemented with, and contrasted to, students' comprehension of information presented aurally. That is, claims differentiating students' linguistic and reasoning capabilities with print media vis à vis aural stimuli could be of use in more fully understanding elementary students' reading comprehension capabilities.

Clearly grounding such claims would require a companion line of assessment argumentation, with aural stimuli and tasks with demands that paralleled those of the reading tasks. We would draw the reading comprehension research mentioned above to develop complementary assessments.

At the other end, an educated adult (postsecondary qualified) is expected to be able to comprehend, learn from, and respond to the full gamut of printed and electronic texts in society, both in familiar and unfamiliar knowledge domains. The design problem here is often deciding what level of coverage of text and task is most valued, at what demand or proficiency level, and what set of such performances is most likely to generalize to other valued reading requirements of adults. (Whether the National Assessment of Educational Progress ought to include Internet literacy in reading has proven controversial, for example.)

Between these bookends, students are exposed to texts and tasks of increasing difficulty. With respect to texts, difficulty can be defined and measured, in part, with respect to linguistic features (see Biber, 1992; Graesser, McNamara, Louwerse, & Cai, 2004; McNamara, Graesser & Louwerse 2012). Readers must continue to develop their knowledge of the language—phonological, orthographic, morphological, vocabulary/semantic, syntactic, metalinguistic and pragmatic knowledge—simply to maintain surface-level gist understanding within limits of attention and working memory for texts of increasing lengths.

In addition, task demands continue to increase as readers are also asked to reason about text more deeply to solve problems. They are asked to build or integrate text information into and with existing memory and knowledge. Both of these requirements can be manipulated (i.e., text and task), and typologies of the demands can be codified. However, both seem to require some threshold levels of intrinsic cognitive capacity, e.g., attention, working memory, phonemic awareness, basic processing speed, and so on. These capacities must themselves become adapted, integrated, and fine tuned into networks governed by the accumulated learning and experience of reading.

The summative snapshots alluded to must take a sampling of skills from this complex network, as Snow and Lohman (1989) argue we should think of it. The resulting scores on such an assessment can reliably indicate whether students are performing satisfactorily in the main, on tasks that are valued and draw upon mixes of widely applicable literacy resources. But systematic coverage and manipulation in a couple hours of assessment per year will not be diagnostic of which aspects of difficulty may be driving performance, much less what steps might be useful in affecting those drivers.

Assessment Arguments for Perceptual, Cognitive Processing Expertise

The phenomenological experience of the skilled reader interacting with text is as a flow of language and meaning. The letters, words, punctuation, morphological and syntactical markers are all invisible (most of the time) to the reader, entering conscious thought only when a novel processing problem—such as decoding a word that has never been seen in print before—requires extra effort and attention. Yet the science of reading suggests that these most fundamental aspects of print are carried out, in every instance, in the brain of the skilled reader (e.g., Rayner, Chace, Slattery, & Ashby, 2006; Sandak, Mencl, Frost, & Pugh 2004).[1]

For the skilled reader, the average fixation rate per word is about a quarter second, for an average silent reading rate of general adult content of about 250 words per minute, though a reader's moment-to-moment rate will be adjusted according to purpose (Rayner et al., 2006). This rate is only possible because of an accumulation of knowledge and processing skill that makes most of the lower-level processes routine operations on familiar stimuli (though this general rate also seems to be roughly tuned to the working memory, attention span, and general language processing rate of humans). This is knowledge accumulated through years and years of experiential practice reading literally millions of words and thousands of texts. The surface level of reading becomes habitual, routine, invisible.

Event-Related Potential (ERP) (Coles & Rugg, 1996) and other neural techniques track the functional and time-based flow of activity as functional networks of the brain encode and recognize orthographic spelling patterns, activate/retrieve word meanings and sound patterns, and syntactically parse phrase and sentence structures (Breznitz, 2005; Perfetti, Wlotko, & Hart, 2005). This surface structure processing is continuously transformed into a text-base meaning model in which key propositions or ideas are generated and maintained in memory to build a higher order memory of the text (W. Kintsch, 1998; van den Broek, Rapp, & Kendeou, 2005).

This processing story is told more precisely and concretely elsewhere in this volume and in the cognitive literature (e.g., Rayner et al., 2006; W. Kintsch, 1998). The key implication for assessment we wish to draw here is that the skilled reader is drawing upon a vast accumulated knowledge base of language and how it is represented in printed forms just in getting the words off the page, and that this operation of fluent reading for basic gist understanding involves a complex orchestration of perceptual and cognitive neural systems that span multiple functional areas of the brain. Conversely, the struggling reader may suffer a cacophony of breakdowns at this print processing stage that interrupt or interfere with the meaning-making system.

In recent years, there has been increasing recognition that students are leaving their elementary grades with poor print processing habits. They do not recognize and learn words efficiently; they exhibit symptoms of slow, effortful reading of continuous text (Daane, Campbell, Grigg, Goodman, & Oranje, 2005; Jenkins, Fuchs, van den Broek, Espin, & Deno, 2003; Katzir et al., 2006; Samuels, 2006; Tannenbaum, Torgesen, & Wagner, 2006).

We suspect that these poor habits not only make arduous the creation of a thoughtful, stable memory representation of challenging new textual information, but also interfere with the accumulation of knowledge about *language as text*, thus, reducing the efficient recognition and processing of orthographic, morphological, syntactic, and other graphemic markers that govern the invisible, fluent flow of reading, and perhaps reducing the sophistication of language skills themselves (regardless of whether the perceptual channel is visual print or auditory).

Thus, while the traditional comprehension tests discussed previously can determine whether a student can fluently read standard texts for basic understanding, they offer scant help for the more challenging possibilities we must then investigate. Screening/diagnostic batteries are therefore being created to detect when persistent surface-level processing inefficiencies may be a root difficulty in struggling readers.

The use of scenarios for such batteries are specific and targeted. The label "screening/diagnostic" denotes that the measures stand somewhere between the continuum of a simple screening measure and a diagnostic. A screener is typically a quick, efficient, and cost-effective test that attempts to maximize precision along one decision point: Is this individual likely to have a specific difficulty? A diagnostic is typically a more reliable, longer measure or set of measures that may explain the nature and depth of a difficulty.

In terms of assessment arguments, the claims of interest concern the knowledge and processes that readers must marshal to produce comprehension— the very knowledge, processes, and coordination that are bundled together in the claims of general reading comprehension tests discussed above. The tasks that comprise screeners and diagnostics must thus be carefully constructed around theories for aspects of processing that comprise reading, in order to focus evidence on claims about these processes or interactions among them.

An Example of a Screener/Diagnostic Battery

Given space limitations, only a brief review of how we are deploying one such battery in practice in middle and secondary schools is described. The batteries we have developed for middle-range readers (grades four through ten) target the surface level of text processing—word decoding and recognition, morphological awareness, basic reading level vocabulary, sentence processing, efficient basic text processing, and basic literal and inferential text meaning (Sabatini & Bruce, in press).

All six of these subtests are computer-administered in about one class period (averaging five to ten minutes per subtest). Each measure has sufficient number of items, however, to achieve reliabilities in the high $r=.80$ range, with intercorrelations among subtests in the $r=.60–.80$ range. There is evidence that that each subtest yields some unique information over the simple summing of their values (Haberman, Sinharay, & Puhan, 2009; Sabatini, Bruce, & Sinharay, 2009). Correlations with previous year state tests average in the r = .50-.7 range.

As each subtest targets only one or two aspects of each level of processing, they are an incomplete measure of the constructs of decoding, word recognition, etc. Thus, they are screeners in that they point to the need for further diagnostics or toward basic intervention packages that broadly target a component skill construct. Their precision is roughly aligned with the current level of precision in our understanding of reading difficulties and interventions that are effective with middle-level readers. At present, this knowledge base is still emerging, so it is not clear yet how even more precise diagnostic measures could be aligned with specific instructional activities (e.g., Edmonds et al., 2009). As our knowledge of instructional techniques improves, so should the specificity of the measures.

The purpose of the battery, then, is to detect, or perhaps more accurately, rule out surface-level processing difficulties in struggling adolescent readers. Skilled readers, defined in our research as readers who score above proficient on state reading tests, typically also score near ceiling on each of the subtests listed above. That is, the tests are not designed to differentiate among skilled readers; the claims they inform are not of interest for readers who have already evidenced capabilities with these processes in concert, and more.

However, struggling readers present a range of performances and profiles in their subtest scores. The battery is typically administered at the beginning of a school year, initially to all the students in a grade level (to ascertain base rates and prevalence of reading difficulties in a school), though thereafter it would be recommended only for known struggling readers, that is, those who have scored below proficient on state tests or otherwise show evidence of poor reading comprehension.

On this type of assessment, a student could score proficient on all of the component reading skills and still be a poor comprehender (as defined by performance on state or other comprehension test). This is a logical possibility. The demands required of students to be thoughtful and reflective about text, to reason with and beyond the text, to learn complex information from texts for specific purposes and to relate to their existing knowledge are not captured in this fifty-minute battery.

In fact, only modest inferences can be made from this battery with respect to the students' capability to perform at these higher level meaning comprehension processes, i.e., students who score low on component skills *typically* score lower on more complex measures of comprehension. However, a more direct test of these skills could be accomplished by allowing a listening accommodation for learners with print processing difficulties.

The variety of higher order reasoning, thinking, and comprehension skills listed previously could be credibly measured with or without the individual's processing of printed text (examples of this approach include Fletcher et al. 2006; Cahalan-Laitusis, Cook, Cline, King, & Sabatini, 2009). In most cases, the poor print reader is also a poor comprehender, even when provided accommodations, but this is clearly not always or necessarily true, as evidenced by readers with visual impairments or highly compensated dyslexics.

CONCLUSION

These are times of great change in the fields of both reading and assessment. Together they portend significant change in the assessment of reading. Deeper understanding of the nature and acquisition of reading proficiency grounds more precise assessment arguments and ways of gathering data to support them. Improved understanding of assessment arguments and methodologies for implementing them help us put the insights from reading science into practice. The result is a view of reading assessment that is more variegated, more situated, and in some cases more challenging to synthesize than traditional reading comprehension testing, but can provide us the tools we need to move research and practice to the next level.

REFERENCES

Atkinson, D. (2002). Toward a sociocognitive approach to second language acquisition. *The Modern Language Journal, 86,* 525–45.

Bachman, L.F. (2005). Building and supporting a case for test use. *Language Assessment Quarterly, 2,* 1–34.

Biber, D. (1992). On the complexity of discourse complexity: A multidimensional analysis. *Discourse Processes, 15,* 133–63.

Breznitz, Z. (2005). *Fluency in reading: Synchronization of processes.* Mahwah, NJ: Lawrence Erlbaum Associates.

Cahalan-Laitusis, C., Cook, L., Cline, F., King, T., & Sabatini, J. P. (2008). *Examining the impact of audio presentation on tests of reading comprehension* (No. RR-08-23). Princeton, NJ: Educational Testing Service.

Claxton, G. (2001). Education for the learning age: A sociocultural approach to learning. In Wells and Claxton (Eds), *Learning for life in the 21st century* (pp. 21–33). Oxford, UK: Blackwell.

Coles, M. G. H., & Rugg, M. D. (1996). Event-related brain potentials: an introduction. In M. D. Rugg & M. G. H. Coles (Eds.), *Electrophysiology of mind: Event-related brain potentials and cognition* (pp. 1–27). Oxford, UK: Oxford University Press.

Daane, M. C., Campbell, J. R., Grigg, W. S., Goodman, M. J., & Oranje, A. (2005). *Fourth-grade students reading aloud: NAEP 2002 special study of oral reading* (No. NCES 2006-469). Washington, D.C.: U.S. Department of Education, Institution of Education Sciences, National Center for Educational Statistics.

Edmonds, M., Vaughn, S., Wexler, J., Reutebuch, C., Cable, A., Tackett, K., & Schnakenberg, J. W. (2009). A synthesis of reading interventions and effects on reading comprehension outcomes for older struggling readers. *Review of Educational Research, 79*, 262–300.

Embretson, S.E. (Ed.) (1985). *Test design: Developments in psychology and psychometrics*. Orlando: Academic Press.

———. (1998). A cognitive design system approach to generating valid tests: Application to abstract reasoning. *Psychological Methods, 3*, 380–96.

Fletcher, J. M., Coulter, W. A., & Reschly, D. J. (2004). Alternative approaches to the definition and identification of learning disabilities: Some questions and answers. *Annals of Dyslexia, 54*, 304–31.

Fletcher, J. M., Denton, C., & Francis, D. J. (2005). Validity of alternative approaches for the identification of learning disabilities: Operationalizing unexpected underachievement. *Journal of Learning Disabilities, 38*, 545–52.

Fletcher, J. M., Francis, D. J., Boudousquie, A., Copeland, K., Young, V., Kalinowski, S., & Vaughn, S. (2006). Effects of accommodations on high stakes testing for students with reading disabilities. *Exceptional Children, 72*, 135–50.

Gee, J. P. (1992). *The social mind: Language, ideology, and social practice*. New York: Bergin & Garvey.

Gorin, J. S., & Embretson, S. E. (2006). Predicting item properties without tryout: Cognitive modeling of paragraph comprehension items. *Applied Psychological Measurement, 30*, 394–411.

Graesser, A. C., McNamara, D. S., Louwerse, M. M., & Cai, Z. Q. (2004). Coh-Metrix: Analysis of text on cohesion and language. *Behavior Research Methods Instruments & Computers, 36*, 193–202.

Haberman, S., Sinharay, S., & Puhan, G. (2009). Reporting subscores for institutions. *British Journal of Mathematical and Statistical Psychology, 62*, 79–95.

Hawkins, J, & Blakeslee, S. (2004). *On intelligence*. New York: Times Books.

Jenkins, J. R., Fuchs, L. S., van den Broek, P., Espin, C., & Deno, S. L. (2003). Accuracy and fluency in list and context reading of skilled and RD groups: Absolute and relative performance levels. *Learning Disabilities: Research & Practice, 18*, 237–45.

Kambe, G., Rayner, K., & Duffy, S. A. (2001). Global context effects on processing lexically ambiguous words: Evidence from eye fixations. *Memory and Cognition, 29*, 363–72.

Kane, M. (1992). An argument-based approach to validation. *Psychological Bulletin, 112*, 527–35.

———. (2006). Validation. In R. J. Brennan (Ed.), *Educational measurement* (4th ed., pp. 18–64). Lanham, MD: Rowman & Littlefield Education.

Katzir, T., Youngsuk, K., Wolf, M., O'Brien, B., Kennedy, B., Lovett, M., & Morris, R. (2006). Reading fluency: The whole is more than the parts. *Annals of Dyslexia, 56*, 51–82.

Kintsch, E. (2005). Comprehension theory as a guide for the design of thoughtful questions. *Topics in Language Disorders, 25,* 51–64.

Kintsch, W. (1998). *Comprehension: A paradigm for cognition.* New York: Cambridge University Press.

Leighton, J. P. & Gierl, M. J. (Eds.) (2007). *Cognitive diagnostic assessment: Theories and applications.* Cambridge: Cambridge University Press.

Linn, R. L. (Ed.). (1989). *Educational measurement* (3rd ed.) New York: American Council on Education/Macmillan.

McNamara, D. S. (Ed.). (2007). *Reading comprehension strategies: Theories, interventions, and technologies.* Mahwah, NJ: Lawrence Erlbaum Associates.

Messick, S. (1989). Validity. In R.L. Linn (Ed.), *Educational measurement* (3rd ed., pp. 13–103). New York: American Council on Education/Macmillan.

Mislevy, R.J. (2006). Cognitive psychology and educational assessment. *Educational Measurement* (4th ed., pp. 257–305). Phoenix, AZ: Greenwood.

———. (2009). Validity from the perspective of model-based reasoning. In R. L. Lissitz (Ed.), *The concept of validity: Revisions, new directions and applications* (pp. 83–108). Charlotte, NC: Information Age Publishing.

Mislevy, R. J., & Haertel, G. (2006). Implications for evidence-centered design for educational assessment. *Educational Measurement: Issues and Practice, 25,* 6–20.

Mislevy, R. J., Steinberg, L. S., & Almond, R. A. (2003). On the structure of educational assessments. *Measurement: Interdisciplinary Research and Perspectives, 1,* 3–67.

McNamara, D. S., Graesser, A., & Louwerse, N. (2012). Sources of text difficulty: Across genres and grades. In J. P. Sabatini, E. Albro, & T. O'Reilly (Eds.), *Measuring up: Advances in how we asses reading ability* (pp. 89–116). Lanham, MD: Rowman & Littlefield Education.

Perfetti, C. A., Wlotko, E. W., & Hart, L. A. (2005). Word learning and individual differences in word learning reflected in event-related potentials. *Journal of Experimental Psychology: Learning, Memory, and Cognition, 31,* 1281–292.

Rayner, K., Chace, K. H., Slattery, T. J., & Ashby, J. (2006). Eye movements as reflections of comprehension processes in reading. *Scientific Studies of Reading, 10,* 241–55.

Rayner, K., Foorman, B. R., Perfetti, C. A., Pesetsky, D., & Seidenberg, M. S. (2001). How psychological science informs the teaching of reading. *Psychological Science in the Public Interest, 2,* 31–74.

Sabatini, J. P. (2009). From health/medical analogies to helping struggling middle school readers: Issues in applying research to practice. In S. Rosenfield & V. Berninger (Eds.), *Translating science-supported instruction into evidence-based practices: Understanding and applying the implementation process* (pp. 285–316). Oxford, UK: Oxford Press.

Sabatini, J. P., & Bruce, K. (in press). *Study Aid and Reading Assistant (SARA): Technical report.* Princeton, NJ: Educational Testing Service.

Sabatini, J. P., Bruce, K., & Sinharay, S. (2009, June). *Developing reading comprehension assessments for struggling readers.* Paper presented at the Institute for Education Sciences Research Conference, Washington, D.C.

Samuels, S. J. (2006). Toward a model of reading fluency. In S. J. Samuels & A. E. Farstrup (Eds.), *What research has to say about fluency instruction* (pp. 24–46). Newark, DE: International Reading Association.

Sandak, R., Mencl, W. E., Frost, S. J., & Pugh, K. R. (2004). The neurobiological basis of skilled and impaired reading: Recent findings and new directions. *Scientific Studies of Reading, 8,* 273–92.

Snow, R. E., & Lohman, D. F. (1989). Implications of cognitive psychology for educational measurement. In R. L. Linn (Ed.), *Educational measurement* (3rd ed., pp. 263–331). New York: American Council on Education/Macmillan.

Strauss, C., & Quinn, N. (1998). *A cognitive theory of cultural meaning.* New York: Cambridge University Press.

Tannenbaum, K. R., Torgesen, J. K., & Wagner, R. K. (2006). Relationships between word knowledge and reading comprehension in third-grade children. *Scientific Studies of Reading, 10,* 381–98.

Tatsuoka, K. K. (1983). Rule space: An approach for dealing with misconceptions based on item response theory. *Journal of Educational Measurement, 20,* 345–54.

Toulmin, S. E. (1958). *The uses of argument.* Cambridge: Cambridge University Press.

van den Broek, P., Rapp, D. N., & Kendeou, P. (2005). Integrating memory-based and constructionist processes in accounts of reading comprehension. *Discourse Processes, 39,* 299–316.

Vellutino, F. R., Fletcher, J. M., Snowling, M. J., & Scanlon, D. M. (2004). Specific reading disability (dyslexia): What have we learned in the past four decades? *Journal of Child Psychiatry, 45,* 2–40.

Vellutino, F. R., Scanlon, D. M., Sipay, E. R., Small, S. G., Pratt, A., Chen, R., & Denckla, M. B. (1996). Cognitive profiles of difficult-to-remediate and readily remediated poor readers: Early intervention as a vehicle for distinguishing between cognitive and experiential deficits as basic causes of specific reading disability. *Journal of Educational Psychology, 88,* 601–38.

Walczyk, J. J., Marsiglia, C. S., Johns, A. K., & Bryan, K. S. (2004). Children's compensations for poorly automated reading skills. *Discourse Processes, 37,* 47–66.

Wayman, M. M., Wallace, T., Wiley, H. I., Ticha, R., & Espin, C. A. (2007). Literature synthesis on curriculum-based measurement in reading. *The Journal of Special Education, 41,* 85–120.

NOTE

1. For example, the eyes move in jumps that average six to twelve letters—about 1.1 words, fixating long enough to take in a span of letters that comprise a content and surrounding function words, then jump again (Rayner et al, 2006). With experience, some peripheral preview information of the coming words is processed as a prime to the semantic system, but little other information is deeply processed (Kambe, Rayner, and Duffy, 2001).

Chapter Eight

Psychological versus Psychometric Dimensionality in Reading Assessment

André A. Rupp

The accumulation of data is not an assessment. (Cates, 1999, p. 638)

INTRODUCTION

The assessment of any particular facet of what can be subsumed under the umbrella terms of "reading," "reading ability," "reading proficiency," or the like can be a daunting task. The focus of this chapter is on one particular aspect in this process: the way in which modern multidimensional measurement models can help support evidentiary assessment narratives about the multidimensional psychological nature of reading processes.

I begin by briefly discussing how reading researchers use different definitional levels of grain size to represent core processes and strategies involved in reading processes. I then discuss evidentiary cornerstones of the current state of knowledge about the challenges in creating reliable and nonredundant subscale scores with the aid of such multidimensional measurement models.

I specifically highlight the theoretical potential and rhetorical pitfalls of a particular class of multidimensional measurement models, so-called *diagnostic classification models* (DCMs) (e.g., Rupp & Templin, 2008; Rupp, Templin, & Henson, 2010), for creating multivariate profiles of readers in this context. A review of simulation and real-data studies that use DCMs and other multidimensional measurement models underscores that it is illusionary to expect that fine-grained multidimensional psychometric representations of reading can be easily created even if well-defined multidimensional psychological representations exist.

THE MULTIDIMENSIONAL PSYCHOLOGICAL
REPRESENTATION OF READING ABILITY

Independent of the measurement model that is used to analyze data from an assessment of reading, understanding precisely which components of a construct are measured by a particular assessment remains one of the foremost methodological challenges for creating coherent integrated assessment narratives. The degree of difficulty of this process rests, in part, on the *theoretical resolution* of a particular assessment and the resulting *definitional grain size* of the individual components of reading processes that are supposed to be represented by distinct components of multidimensional measurement models.

Representing Reading Processes at Different Levels of Grain Size

Of course, grain size is a relative notion, though not an arbitrary one. Hence, the differentiation of the cognitive grain size from "coarse grained" to "fine grained" is mediated by the educational assessment context. For example, understanding the neurological bases for cognitive processes involved in reading or empirically investigating differential hypotheses about the arrangement of the enabling mental architecture (e.g., the structure of the mental lexicon) is very different from identifying key component skills such as understanding sentence-level inferences or basic grammatical structures on a global assessment of reading ability. However, neither set of purposes is directly indicative of what the definitional grain size of any elements of these studies would be that one would seek to represent with particular measurement models.

As Stanovich (2003) summarizes, the cognitively based literature on reading has seen remarkable progress in the past decades; researchers have a rather comprehensive understanding about the interaction of key subskills that are relevant for successful and effective reading for different purposes. Open research questions about issues such as optimizing procedures for the diagnosis and remediation of reading deficiencies, monitoring long-term development of reading comprehension, and investigating neurological bases of impairments of subskills nevertheless abound.

But a few facts about the cognitive processes of reading comprehension seem to be agreed upon by most experts. For a description of the current knowledge state, one may read the introduction to any carefully designed study or research program of reading comprehension, in which the authors talk eloquently about the complex process and its subskills (e.g., Enright et al., 2000; Francis et al., 2006; Lesaux, Rupp, & Siegel, 2007; O'Reilly &

Sheehan, 2009; Sadoski & Paivio, 2007; Sheehan & O'Reilly, 2011; Vellutino, Tunmer, Jaccard, & Chen, 2007).

For the purpose of this chapter I found it useful to distinguish broadly between more *basic reading processes* and more *advanced reading comprehension* processes. For example, the relationship between basic subskills of reading and basic reading ability, summarized by the *Southwest Educational Development Laboratory* group in its cognitive assessment framework (www.sedl.org/reading/framework), is reproduced in Figure 8.1. It shows that successful reading comprehension firmly rests on language comprehension and decoding skills, which, in turn, rest on background knowledge and linguistic knowledge as well as cipher knowledge and lexical knowledge. These, in turn, rest on knowledge in phonology, syntax, and semantics as well as phoneme awareness, knowledge of the alphabetic principle, letter knowledge, and concepts about print.

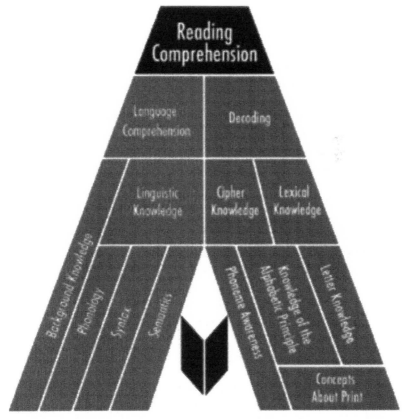

Figure 8.1.   A visual representation of a cognitive framework for basic reading.

Of course, the degree to which learners need to draw on these skills depends on the interaction between characteristics of the tasks and the learners. From a cognitive assessment perspective, such an organization is helpful as it allows one to broadly classify existing assessments as to which aspect of reading ability they target. This is done, for example, in the SEDL database for assessments targeted primarily at pre-K to grade 3, with some available for higher grades as well.

In contrast, more nuanced models of comprehension assessment include relationships between subskills of reading, reading strategies, and knowledge of text conventions for reading comprehension (Deane, Sabatini, & O'Reilly, 2011; O'Reilly & Sheehan, 2009; Sheehan & O'Reilly, 2011). That is, basic reading skills are assumed to have been mastered to a minimally sufficient degree for readers to engage at least somewhat successfully in the more advanced reading comprehension processes.

Put differently, assessment inferences about readers' abilities to perform different kinds of more advanced reading comprehension tasks are most important when the focus of reading assessment is on *reading-to-learn* (i.e., building mental representations of texts) and *reading-to-do* (i.e., using print information to perform tasks).

In contrast, assessment inferences about readers' mastery of subskills of reading and their ability to effectively draw on basic mental capacities are most important when the focus is on *learning-to-read* (i.e., developing the foundational skills for processing text). I note here that the interactions of different basic reading and more advanced reading comprehension skills are certainly rather complex for any given reading context, reading purpose, and reader profile, and I will leave nuanced discussions of these interactions to other authors of this volume.

Assessing Reading Processes at Different Levels of Grain Size

Assessments that allow for the creation of reader profiles based on more narrowly defined cognitive skills are clearly more informative about the basic cognitive processes of reading. Consequently, they can only provide reliable information about small aspects of the global construct of reading comprehension. In contrast, assessments that allow for the creation of reader profiles based on more coarsely defined cognitive skills cover broader aspects of a complex construct, but leave the empirical connections between individual skills and actual cognitive processes much more undifferentiated.

Moreover, it is clear that more complex reading comprehension skills such as "understand the literal meaning of text," "infer relations among concepts," "access relevant background knowledge," and "understand difficult vocabulary/literary terms" are useful to characterize reading performance for, say, expository texts that are targeted in complexity from middle schoolers to graduate students. However, this does not necessarily imply that a particular representation of these skills in statistical models (e.g., an encoding of "mastery" versus "nonmastery" for individual skills) yields a meaningful interpretational grounding for characterizing performance differences of readers.

As Leighton and Gierl (2007) state, many assessments at a fine grain size are necessary to arrive at a more complete fine-grained understanding of the different aspects of a complex construct such as reading. However, resources such as testing time, personnel, and money are, of course, limited in real-life assessment contexts, which leads to a frequently observed conundrum in modern-day standardized achievement testing: Policy makers often wish to describe individual readers at once in terms of overall levels of reading comprehension, particular types of reading comprehension, and various subskills of reading with the least amount of resources possible; ideally, with one short "diagnostic" assessment.

Many current standards-based assessment policies either explicitly state such a goal or implicitly suggest it (e.g., Rupp, Vock, Harsch, & Köller, 2008; see Rupp, Lesaux, & Siegel, 2006). Similarly, educators seem to demand highly diagnostic information despite generally despising the current increase of standardized testing (see, e.g., Huff & Goodman, 2007).

However, assessments cannot fulfill empirical demands at different levels jointly with the same degree of accuracy and precision. As a resort of last hope, so to speak, assessment designers then often turn to modern psychometric measurement models in the hope that they can somehow empirically "make up" for conflicting design and interpretation goals. Not surprisingly, this is typically met with failure.

Implications of Representational Levels for Psychometric Representations of Reading Processes

While many of the above points seem intuitively clear to most researchers, the important, and sometimes overlooked, implication is that a particular cognitive framework for reading at a particular level of definitional grain size can have multiple potential psychometric representations via measurement models.

In order to arrive at a comprehensive picture of the developing reading ability of an individual cross-sectionally or longitudinally over time, multiple pieces of evidence from different assessments that target different aspects of reading ability with different degrees of resolution are needed. In order to ground this comprehensive picture empirically, an alignment of the interpretations from the different subscales of the measurement models that are used to model the data from the different reading assessments are needed.

Another important aspect that affects the nature of assessment inferences, apart from the definitional grain size of the involved components in a cognitive model of task performance, is the mapping of the observable score variables from the assessment onto the unobservable latent variables that reflect these components.

Put simply, having a fine-grained cognitive resolution is a necessary, but not sufficient, condition to provide meaningful fine-grained inferences about the cognitive processes of readers. For example, it is also necessary to specify whether different cognitive components interact in a *compensatory* or *non-compensatory* manner (i.e., whether the mastery of one skill can make up for the lack of mastery of another subskill) and whether there are *conditional relationships* between individual components such as ceiling or floor effects for their mastery.

In sum, reading is clearly a *psychologically multidimensional construct* in that multiple subskills and reading strategies are engaged in any particular reading task at any given point in time by any given reader. Consequently, applied practitioners often expect that the scoring of the performance of readers on assessments of reading should lead almost "naturally" to multidimensional score profiles that are easily and reliably interpretable.

As McNamara (1996) reminded us many years ago, however, psychological multidimensionality does not equal psychometric multidimensionality. As we shall see in the next section of this chapter, the development of multiple measurement dimensions that provide reliable and nonredundant information about individual components of reading ability via appropriate multidimensional measurement models is a demanding and often daunting task.

THE MULTIDIMENSIONAL PSYCHOMETRIC REPRESENTATION OF READING ABILITY

In the modern psychometric literature, the demand for an increased precision of diagnostic feedback at some definitional level of grain size is viewed as the problem of creating *reliable* and *nonredundant subscale scores*. There are many tools in the current psychometric toolbox with which subscale scores can be created (e.g., Tate, 2003; see also Martineau et al., 2007). Measurement models for creating subscale scores that place stronger demands on the data structure include *latent variables* whose distributions or individual values need to be statistically estimated. These models are typically based on either *classical test theory* (CTT) (e.g., Lord & Novick, 1968; Thissen &

Wainer, 2001) or *item response theory* (IRT) (e.g., de Ayala, 2009; Embretson & Reise, 2000).

Choosing a Measurement Model for Representing Reading Processes

The choice for a latent-variable framework is statistically driven in that the highest degree of psychometric and inferential power is achieved when fully parametric measurement models are used. For assessment data that are discrete (i.e., dichotomous or polytomous), multiple unidimensional CTT or IRT models are often used separately for each targeted subscale (e.g., Sheng & Wikle, 2007) but there has also been an increase in the direct use of *multidimensional IRT* models in practice (e.g., Ackerman, Gierl, & Walker, 2003; Reckase, 2009; te Marvelde, Glas, van Landeghem, & van Damme, 2006).

Notably, scoring individuals within a *confirmatory factor analysis (CFA)* or *structural equation modeling (SEM)* framework for discrete response data can work equally well under certain circumstances (e.g., Kline, 2010; McDonald, 1999; Thissen & Wainer, 2001). However, since the creation and reporting of subscale scores is not the primary motivation for using CFAs or SEMs, which are more frequently used to test construct relationships rather than scoring individuals, they are rarely used for the creation of multidimensional reading profiles that are reported back to individual readers.

Empirical Challenges for Creating Multidimensional Representations of Reading Processes

Independent of which measurement model is chosen, research consistently finds that many assessments within a single domain sturdily resist analysts' efforts to carve out multidimensional structures empirically. Subscale scores are typically highly correlated despite multidimensional assessment designs as reflected in their *tables of specification* (e.g., Haladyna & Kramer, 2004; Wainer, Sheehan, & Wang, 2000).

Moreover, even if multiple subscale scores can be constructed, they are often less reliable than the unidimensional total test scores or latent variable scores (e.g., Monaghan, 2006; Sinharay, Haberman, & Puhan, 2007). *Empirical Bayes techniques* that capitalize on the joint information across scales for each subscale can improve reliability estimates vis-à-vis CTT methods (e.g., Thissen & Wainer, 2001; Wainer et al., 2000), but subscale scores typically remain highly correlated and only moderately reliable (e.g., Haberman & Sinharay, 2009; Haberman, Sinharay, & Puhan, 2009; Puhan, Sinharay, Haberman, & Larkin, 2010).

Potentials and Pitfalls of DCMs for Creating Multidimensional Profiles of Reading

As a potential pathway toward remedying some of the shortcomings listed above, methodologists in the last twenty years or so have intensely investigated the theoretical potential of multidimensional measurement models that may be able to provide more reliable and less correlated subscale scores in a more efficient manner. These models are known collectively as *cognitive diagnosis models* or *diagnostic classification models* (DCMs) (e.g., diBello, Roussos, & Stout, 2007; Fu & Li, 2007; Hartz, 2002; Rupp & Mislevy, 2007; Rupp & Templin, 2008; Rupp et al., 2010; see also the special 2007 issue of *Journal of Educational Measurement*).

Technically speaking, these models are extensions of multidimensional latent variable models developed within IRT and latent class frameworks (e.g., Dayton, 2008; Haertel, 1989). Most importantly, they contain *discrete latent variables* that allow for a *statistically driven classification* of readers (e.g., for each subskill it is determined whether the reader has mastered it or not) and can handle *complex assessment designs* wherein each reading task measures multiple subskills with relative ease.

Some DCMs are only applicable for certain combinations of response variable and latent variable scales, while others are more flexible. Researchers have recently shown how many models can be re-expressed as members of a larger family of models that blurs historical distinctions of model classes based on whether subskills interacted in a noncompensatory or compensatory manner.

For example, von Davier (2005, 2010), Henson, Templin, & Willse (2009), and de la Torre (2008, 2011) use an extended *generalized linear and nonlinear mixed model* approach (e.g., de Boeck & Wilson, 2004; Rijmen, Tuerlinckx, de Boeck, & Kuppen, 2003; Skrondal & Rabe-Hesketh, 2004) that uses a linear predictor function to represent a wide variety of compensatory as well as noncompensatory DCMs (see Templin & Rupp, in press).

Specialists of DCMs argue that they are best used in formative assessment settings or for clinical diagnosis purposes (e.g., diBello et al., 2007; Leighton & Gierl, 2007; Templin & Henson, 2006). However, just like any other fully parameterized multidimensional modeling approach, more complex models generally require large respondent sample sizes for a trustworthy calibration of item operating characteristics (e.g., difficulty, discrimination, and guessing parameters) and large number of items per measurement dimension for trustworthy scaling of respondents.

It is generally true that DCMs require fewer items per dimension than multidimensional models with continuous latent variables to achieve the same level of reliability (Templin & Henson, 2006). Bayesian estimation methods can further alleviate this estimation challenge to same degree if experts are able to specify likely values for item and respondent parameters based on experience and research. As data come in, model-fitting tools can be used to improve the structure of the model further, and Bayesian updating can be used to improve the parameter estimates within the models.

Nevertheless, I would argue that is better to be more cautious when making inferences about multiple measurement dimensions rather than to believe that having only, say, two or three items per dimension leads to trustworthy inferences about cognitive processes involved in basic or more advanced reading comprehension.

Moreover, if specialists want to eventually use simpler scoring rules for subscales and classification based on such models in real-life settings, then these models need to be calibrated and cross-validated on multiple large samples first to lend credibility to such scoring processes.

I believe it is fair to say that comprehensive validation programs for DCMs have, so far, not appeared in the literature even though a few examples that reflect best practices in more traditional large-scale modeling contexts have recently been published (e.g., Kunina-Habenicht, Rupp, & Wilhelm, 2009; Templin & Henson, 2006; see also Levy & Mislevy, 2004).

To overcome some of the application limitations of fully parametric measurement models, concerted research activities have recently been extended to investigate how simpler classification algorithms and data-mining tools can be used to achieve similar multidimensional scaling objectives (e.g., Ayers, Nugent, & Dean, 2008, 2009).

These methods place fewer demands on the data structures to which they are applied due to their algorithmic nature and can perform similar to fully parametric DCMs under certain conditions (e.g., Willse, Henson, & Templin, 2008; Chiu, 2008) at the expense of losing some richness in the inferential machinery. Their development is conceptually aligned with hybrid methods that rely on parametric and nonparametric components; prominent examples include the *rule-space methodology* (e.g., Tatsuoka, 2009) and the *attribute hierarchy method* (e.g., Gierl, Leighton, & Hunka, 2007).

The Importance of Scientific Styles in the Assessment of Reading

It is worth commenting on a somewhat philosophical aspect of the reasoning process with multidimensional measurement models. The objective of cognitively grounded analyses of data from reading assessments is to deconstruct the underlying cognitive process of reading comprehension into its subcomponents in one form or another informed by research from psycholinguistics, cognitive psychology, and reading assessment. This perspective reflects a style of science that seeks correspondence, analytic reductionism, probabilistic predictions, robust process explanations, and consilience (Stanovich, 2003).

Consequently, it is typically useful to situate debates among specialists about whether an application of multidimensional measurement models is appropriate for a given measurement context within a discussion of their individual scientific styles and the resulting beliefs about evidentiary systems. Similarly, an investigation of the value of the theory that such models operationalize is key to judging the contribution that their application makes not only to the discipline of measurement but also the discipline of the scientific study of reading. As Pete Richerson and Robert Boyd state, "to replace a world you do not understand by a model of the world you do not understand is no advance" (cited in Smith, 2000, p.46).

CONCLUSION

In sum, the current repertoire of psychometric measurement models from different modeling frameworks, both parametric and nonparametric, is rich. Nevertheless, these models do not possess any "magical empirical powers" that allow them to empirically carve out highly multidimensional profiles of readers at a fine grain size in the absence of well-designed reading assessments.

While it is true that measurement models with discrete latent variables such as DCMs can produce more reliable profiles with fewer reading tasks—since the differentiation between different readers is coarser—structurally similar models with continuous latent variables from IRT generally lead to very similar multidimensional representations (see Haberman, von Davier, and Lee, 2008, for a technical argument and Kunina, Rupp, and Wilhelm, 2009, for an empirical illustration from the domain of arithmetic ability).

Table 8.1 summarizes the key design features of selected recent studies that have used multidimensional IRT models to create multidimensional profiles, while Table 8.2 summarizes the key design features for selected recent studies that have used DCMs; note that the cited studies are mostly not from the domain of reading due to a dearth of applications with these models in this domain. The overall picture that emerges from these tables is that most application contexts with multidimensional IRT models lead to the creation of around two or three separable dimensions that are reasonably highly correlated nevertheless. In contrast, researchers have applied higher-dimensional DCMs to create dimensions that lead to subscale scores with lower correlations, but these are mostly statistical artifacts due to the fact that each dimension is characterized by two, or at most a few, proficiency score values. Furthermore, it should

Table 8.1. Summary of key design characteristics of studies with compensatory multidimensional IRT models.

Type	First Author	Year	# of Items	# of Respondents	# of Dimensions	Attribute Correlations	# of Model Parameters
Simulated Data	Bolt	2003	25, 50	1000, 3000	2	0, .3, .6	2
	Finch	2006	15, 30, 60	250, 1000, 2000	2	0, .3, .5, .8	2
	Finch	2005	15, 30, 60	1000, 2000	2	0, .3, .8, .95	2
	Li	2000	40	1000, 2000, 4000	2	0	2
	Oshima	1997	40	2000	2	0, .5	2
	Oshima	2000	40	NG	2	.4, .5, .7	2
	Ricker	2007	68, 120	2000	2	0, .3, .7	2
	Sheng	2007	41	1000	2	0, .6, .8	2
	Adams	1998	20, 40	300, 700	2, 3	0, .5	1
	Li	2006	60	13000	3	0, .5, .7	2
	Yao	2007	60	1000, 3000, 6000	4	0, .1, .3, .5,, .7, .9	3
	de la Torre	2004	10, 30, 50	1000	2, 5	0, .4, .7, .9	3
	Tate	2004	60	1000	2, 3, 4, 5	0, .2, .4, .6, .8, .9, .95	1
Real Data	Ackerman	2003	35	6000	2	.84	2
	Beretvas	2004	17	5652	2	.49	3
	Bolt	2003	31	3000	2	.67	2
	Kupermintz	1997	40	2554	2	.67	3
	Ricker	2007	100, 120	4226, 3877	2	.21 - .55	2
	Rijmen	2005	24	316	2	0.78	1
	Hartig*	2008	15, 21	9778	2	.91	2
	Sheng	2007	NG	1231	2	.82	2
	Adams	1998	21	NG	3	.85 – .97	1
	de la Torre	2005	90	2255	4	.66 – .89	3
	Haladyna	2004	400	6390	4	.83 – .94	3
	Finch	2005	36	1190	6	.74 – .95	2
	Reckase	1997	40	1635	2, 6	NG	3

NG = not given. * = mean values per person for each dimension and total number of respondents based on a complex booklet design.

Table 8.2. Summary of key design characteristics of studies with DCMs

Type	First Author	Year	# of Items	# of Respondents	# of Dimensions	Attribute Correlations	Mastery Proportions
Simulated Data	Maris	1999	20, 40	100, 250, 1000, 2500	2, 4	.40 – .70	.40 – .70
	Bolt	2004	20	500, 1000, 5000	4	.29 – .82	.30 – .65
	Fu	2008	20	500, 2000	4	.37 – .86	.30 – .90
	Liu	2009	30 – 90	1000, 1200	5	0	.50
	von Davier	2005	36	2880	4	NG	.50
	de la Torre	2007	30	5000	5	NG	NG
	Roussos	2004	40	2000, 6000	6	.62 – .91	.32 – .60
	Hartz	2000	40	1500	7	.09 – .84	.30 – .65
	Henson	2005	300	10000	3, 8	.00 – .50	.50
	Templin	2005	40	3000	7, 8	.29	.41 – .60
	Karelitz	2004	48	2000	9 – 15	0	.50
Real Data	Henson	2008	30	2922	3	.61 – .76	.41 – .66
	Maris	1999	37	595	3	NG	< .72
	Templin	2005	41	1372	4	.38 – .90	.34 – .65
	von Davier	2005	34, 39, 40	419, 2720	4	.42 – .96	0.5
	Junker	2001	9	417	6	NG	NG
	Levy	2004	28+	216	6	NG	NG
	Liu	2009	30	2922	3	NG	NG
	Gierl	2007	250	NG	8	NG	NG
	de la Torre	2007	90	3823	9	NG	NG
	Jang	2005	37, 38	1372, 1331	9	NG	NG
	Templin	2006	41	128	10	.17 – .28	.08 – .41
	Kunina	2009	66	464	5	.39 – .95	.37 – .69
	Hartz	2000	40, 39	1836, 3329, 585	15 – 17	NG	.30 – .70
	Birenbaum	2004	162	2092, 2371, 4411	23	NG	.26 – .95
	Buck	1998	19	13000	23	NG	.34 – .98

NG = not given.

be noted that very few thorough investigations of model-data fit at different levels (i.e., global, item, and person) are currently published for these models (but see Liu, Douglas, & Henson, 2009, and Kunina-Habenicht, Rupp, & Wilhelm, 2010 for first steps). Yet such an assessment is crucial to determine the trustworthiness of any interpretations about reading processes that are drawn about the respondents on the basis of the estimated model parameters.

Thus, it may be possible to create low-dimensional representations of reading abilities using multidimensional measurement models when the dimensions represent reasonably distinct subcomponents of reading that are defined at a coarser level of grain size. At the same time, it will generally be illusionary to expect that high-dimensional representations of reading abilities can be easily constructed using multidimensional measurement models when the dimensions represent closely related subskills that are defined at a finer level of grain size. That is, creating multidimensional psychometric profiles for readers is a challenging modeling task even when the multidimensional psychological nature of reading can be well understood.

REFERENCES

Ackerman, T. A., Gierl, M. J., & Walker, C. M. (2003). Using multidimensional item response theory to evaluate educational and psychological tests. *Educational Measurement: Issues and Practice, 22,* 37–53.

Ayers, E., Nugent, R., & Dean, N. (2008, June). Skill set profile clustering based on student capability vectors computed from online tutoring data. Presented at the Annual Educational Data Mining Conference, Montreal, Quebec.

———. (2009, July). A comparison of student skill knowledge estimates. Presented at the Annual Educational Data Mining Conference, Cordoba, Spain.

Cates, J. A. (1999). The art of assessment in psychology: Ethics, expertise, and validity. *Journal of Clinical Psychology, 55,* 631–41.

Chiu, C.-Y. (2008). Cluster analysis for cognitive diagnosis: Theory and applications. (Unpublished doctoral dissertation) University of Illinois at Urbana-Champaign, Urbana-Champaign, IL.

Dayton, C. M. (2008). Introduction to latent class analysis. In S. Menard (Ed.), *Handbook of longitudinal research: Design, measurement, and analysis* (pp. 357–72). San Diego, CA: Elsevier.

de Ayala, R. J. (2009). *Principles and practice of item response theory.* New York: Guilford Press.

De Boeck, P., & Wilson, M. (2004). *Explanatory item response theory models: A generalized linear and nonlinear approach.* New York: Springer.

de la Torre, J. (2008, July). The generalized DINA model. Paper presented at the annual International Meeting of the Psychometric Society (IMPS), Durham, NH.

———. (in 2011). The generalized DINA model framework. *Psychometrika, 76,* 179–199.

Deane, P., Sabatini, J., & O'Reilly, T. (2011). *English language arts literacy framework.* Princeton, NJ: Educational Testing Service.

di Bello, L., Roussos, L. A., & Stout, W. (2007). Review of cognitively diagnostic assessment and a summary of psychometric models. In C. V. Rao & S. Sinharay (Eds.), *Handbook of statistics: Psychometrics* (Vol. 26, pp. 979–1027). Amsterdam, The Netherlands: Elsevier.

Embretson, S. E., & Reise, S. P. (2000). *Item response theory for psychologists.* Mahwah, NJ: Lawrence Erlbaum Associates.

Enright, M. K., Grabe, W., Koda, K., Mosenthal, P., Mulcahy-Ernt, P., & Schedl, M. (2000). TOEFL 2000 Reading Framework: A working paper (TOEFL Monograph Series Nr. MS-17). Princteton, NJ: Educational Testing Service.

Francis, D. J., Snow, C. E., August, D., Carlson, C. D., Miller, J., & Iglesias, A. (2006). Measures of reading comprehension: A latent variable analysis of the diagnostic assessment of reading comprehension. *Scientific Studies of Reading, 10,* 301–22.

Fu, J., & Li, Y. (2007, April). An integrated review of cognitively diagnostic psychometric models. Paper presented at the annual meeting of the National Council on Measurement in Education, Chicago, IL.

Gierl, M. J., Leighton, J. P., & Hunka, S. M. (2007). Using the attribute hierarchy method to make diagnostic inferences about respondents' cognitive skills. In J. P. Leighton & M. J. Gierl (Eds.), *Cognitive diagnostic assessment for education: Theory and applications* (pp. 242–74). Cambridge, UK: Cambridge University Press.

Haberman, S., & Sinharay, S. (2009). Reporting of subscores using multidimensional item response theory. *Psychometrika, 75,* 209–27.

Haberman, S., Sinharay, S., & Puhan, G. (2009). Reporting subscores for institutions. *British Journal of Mathematical and Statistical Psychology, 62,* 79–95.

Haberman, S. J., von Davier, M., & Lee, Y.-J. (2008). Comparison of multidimensional item response models: Multivariate normal ability distributions versus multivariate polytomous ability distributions (Research Report No. RR-08-45). Princeton, NJ: Educational Testing Service.

Haertel, E. H. (1989). Using restricted latent class models to map the skill structure of achievement items. *Journal of Educational Measurement, 26,* 301–23.

Haladyna, T. M., & Kramer, G. A. (2004). The validity of subscale scores for a credentialing test. *Evaluation and the Health Professions, 27,* 349–68.

Hartz, S. M. (2002). A Bayesian framework for the unified model for assessing cognitive abilities: Blending theory with practicality (unpublished doctoral dissertation). University of Illinois at Urbana-Champaign.

Henson, R., Templin, J., & Willse, J. (2009). Defining a family of cognitive diagnosis models using log-linear models with latent variables. *Psychometrika, 74,* 191–210.

Huff, K., & Goodman, D. P. (2007). The demand for cognitive diagnostic assessment. In J. P. Leighton & M. J. Gierl (Eds.), *Cognitive diagnostic assessment for education: Theory and applications* (pp. 19–60). Cambridge: Cambridge University Press.

Jang, E. E., & Roussos, L. (2007). An investigation into the dimensionality of TOEFL using conditional covariance-based nonparametric approach. *Journal of Educational Measurement, 44,* 1–22.

Journal of Educational Measurement (2007, Volume 4). Special issue on IRT-based cognitive diagnostic models and related methods.

Kline, R. (2010). *Principles and practice of structural equation modeling* (3rd ed.). New York: Guilford Press.

Kunina-Habenicht, O., Rupp, A. A., & Wilhelm, O. (2009). A practical illustration of multidimensional diagnostic skills profiling: Comparing results from confirmatory factor analysis and diagnostic classification models. *Studies in Educational Evaluation, 35*, 64–70.

———. (2010). An empirical investigation of four different item-fit indices for diagnostic classification models to different types of model misspecification. Manuscript under review.

Leighton, J. P., & Gierl, M. J. (2007). *Diagnostic assessment for education: Methods and applications.* Cambridge, UK: Cambridge University Press.

Lesaux, N. K., Rupp, A. A., & Siegel, L. S. (2007). Growth in reading skills of children from diverse linguistic backgrounds: Findings from a 5-year longitudinal study. *Journal of Educational Psychology, 99*, 821–34.

Levy, R., & Mislevy, R. J. (2004). Specifying and refining a measurement model for a computer-based interactive assessment. *International Journal of Testing, 4*, 333–69.

Liu, Y., Douglas, J. A., & Henson, R. A. (2009). Testing person fit in cognitive diagnosis. *Applied Psychological Measurement, 33*, 579–98.

Lord, F. M., & Novick, M. R. (1968). *Statistical theories of mental test scores.* New York: Information Age Publishing.

Martineau, J. A., Subedi, D. R., Ward, K. H., Li, T., Lu, Y., Diao, Q., & Li, X. (2007). Non-linear trajectories through multidimensional content spaces: An examination of psychometric claims of unidimensionality, linearity, and interval-level measurement. In: R. W. Lissitz (Ed.), *Assessing and modelling cognitive development in school* (pp. 96–142). Maple Grove, MN: JAM Press.

McDonald, R. P. (1999). *Test theory: A unified treatment.* Mahwah, NJ: Lawrence Erlbaum Associates.

McNamara, T. F. (1996). *Measuring second language performance.* New York: Addison Wesley Longman.

Monaghan, W. (2006). The facts about subscale scores. *R&D Connections.* Princeton, NJ: Educational Testing Service.

O'Reilly & Sheehan, K. (2009). *Cognitively based assessment of, for, and as learning: A 21st century approach for assessing reading competency* (RM-09-04). Princeton: NJ: Educational Testing Service.

Puhan, G., Sinharay, S., Haberman, S., & Larkin, K. (2010). The utility of augmented subscores in licensure exams: An evaluation of methods using empirical data. *Applied Measurement in Education, 23*, 266–85.

Reckase, M. (2009). *Multidimensional item response theory.* New York: Springer.

Rijmen, F., Tuerlickx, F., De Boeck, P., & Kuppens, P. (2003). A nonlinear mixed model framework for item response theory. *Psychological Methods, 8*, 185–205.

Rupp, A. A., Lesaux, N. K., & Siegel, L. S. (2006). Meeting expectations? Empirical investigations of a standards-based assessment of reading comprehension. *Educational Evaluation and Policy Analysis, 28*, 315–33.

Rupp, A. A., & Mislevy, R. J. (2007). Cognitive foundations of structured item response theory models. In J. P. Leighton & M. J. Gierl (Eds.), *Cognitive diagnostic assessment for education: Theory and applications* (pp. 205–41). Cambridge: Cambridge University Press.

Rupp, A. A., & Templin, J. (2008). Unique characteristics of cognitive diagnosis models: A comprehensive review of the current state-of-the-art. *Measurement: Interdisciplinary Research and Perspectives, 6,* 219-262.

Rupp, A. A., Templin, J., & Henson, R. (2010). *Diagnostic measurement: Theory, methods, and applications.* New York: Guilford Press.

Rupp, A. A., Vock, M., Harsch, C., & Köller, O. (2008). *Developing standards-based assessment tasks for English as a first foreign language: Context, processes, and outcomes in Germany.* Münster, Germany: Waxmann.

Sadoski, M., & Paivio, A. (2007). Toward a unified theory of reading. *Scientific Studies of Reading, 11,* 337–56.

Sheehan, K. & O'Reilly, T. (2011). *The CBAl reading assessment: An approach for balancing measurement and learning goals.* (RR-11-21). Princeton, NJ: Educational Testing Service.

Sheng, Y., & Wikle, C. K. (2007). Comparing multidimensional and unidimensional item response theory models. *Educational and Psychological Measurement, 67,* 899–919.

Sinharay, S., Haberman, S., & Puhan, G. (2007) Subscale scores based on classical test theory: To report or not to report. *Educational Measurement: Issues and Practice 26,* 21–28.

Skrondal, A., & Rabe-Hesketh, S. (2004). *Generalized latent variable modeling: Multilevel, longitudinal, and structural equation models.* New York: Chapman & Hall / CRC.

Smith, M. (2000, December 21). Review of the book "The century of the gene." *New York Review of Books, 47,* 43–46.

Stanovich, K. E. (2003). Understanding the styles of science in the study of reading. *Scientific Studies of Reading, 7,* 105–26.

Tate, R. (2003). A comparison of selected empirical methods for assessing the structure or responses to test items. *Applied Psychological Measurement, 27,* 159–203.

Tatsuoka, K. K. (2009). *Cognitive assessment: An introduction to the rule-space method.* Florence, KY: Routledge.

te Marvelde, J. M., Glas, C. A. W., van Landeghem, G., & van Damme, J. (2006). Applications of multidimensional item response theory models to longitudinal data. *Educational and Psychological Measurement, 66,* 5–34.

Templin, J. L., & Henson, R. A. (2006). Measurement of psychological disorders using cognitive diagnosis models. *Psychological Methods, 11,* 287–305.

Templin, J., & Rupp, A. A. (in press). On the origins of a statistical species: The evolution of diagnostic classification models within the psychometric taxonomy. In G. Macready & G. Hancock (Eds.), *A Festschrift in honor of C. Mitchell Dayton.* Charlotte, NC: Information Age Publishing.

Thissen, D., & Wainer, H. (Eds.). (2001). *Test scoring.* Mahwah, NJ: Lawrence Erlbaum Associates.

Vellutino, F. R., Tunmer, W. E., Jaccard, J. J., & Chen, R. (2007). Components of reading ability: Multivariate evidence for a convergent skills model of reading development. *Scientific Studies of Reading, 11,* 3–32.

von Davier, M. (2005). *A general diagnostic model applied to language testing data* (Research Report No. RR-05-16). Princeton, NJ: Educational Testing Service.

———. (2010). Hierarchical mixtures of diagnostic models. *Psychological Test and Assessment Modeling, 52,* 8–28.

Wainer, H., Sheehan, K. M., & Wang, X. (2000). Some paths toward making Praxis scores more useful. *Journal of Educational Measurement, 37,* 113–40.

Willse, J., Templin, J., & Henson, R. (2008, March). *K-means with latent class refinement: Cognitive diagnosis with few assumptions.* Paper presented at the annual meeting of the National Council on Measurement in Education, New York.

Conclusion

Moving Forward on Reading Assessment

Arthur Graesser & Xiangen Hu

One vision of the future is that computers will guide most phases of instruction, reading comprehension, formative assessment, and testing. We live in a world where many/most students prefer interacting with computers during learning than listening to teachers lecture. Computer technologies are ubiquitous in our world so we have some opportunities to substantially improve reading assessments. We can record what particular students read at particular points in time in both academic and informal settings.

The rich array of data can be mined at varying grain sizes over months or years, yielding thousands or even millions of data points for individual readers. This vision is very different than an efficient, two-hour multiple-choice paper and pencil test on a critical day when high school students take the SAT test on verbal comprehension.

My research background is somewhat unusual so I should clarify the lens through which I perceive reading assessment. After being trained in the 1970s in cognitive psychology and discourse processing, my research contributions focused on cognitive models of text comprehension, inferences, question asking, question answering, learning, and emotions. I have always participated in interdisciplinary research teams that embrace the fields of education, computer science, engineering, and quantitative methods. I have always been fascinated with technologies at the intersection of psychological theory.

As a consequence, my colleagues and I have developed and tested computerized learning environments (such as AutoTutor, MetaTutor), language and discourse technologies with advances in computational linguistics (such as QUAID, QUEST, and Coh-Metrix), eye tracking technologies that record events while individuals read text and multimedia, and multichannel communication technologies that infer learner emotions from dialogue, speech parameters, facial expressions, and body posture.

153

I have paid my dues in professional service (time and time again) as editor of two journals (*Discourse Processes* and *Journal of Educational Psychology*) and presidents of societies (Society for Text and Discourse, Artificial Intelligence in Education, and the Society for the Empirical Studies of Literature). I have participated in several research teams with the College Board and Educational Testing Service that have had the goal of improving the Verbal Comprehension components of psychometric tests (such as the SAT). These experiences provide a unique context for critiquing existing assessments of reading and speculating on improved assessments in the future.

Contributors to this workshop are presumably convinced that there will be dramatic improvements in methods to assess reading skills and comprehension. That definitely was the case when I served on the professional teams to improve verbal comprehension tests. Some of the teams had cognitive researchers analyze items on multiple choice tests by identifying the cognitive skills that were reflected in the question items, keys, and distracters. The hope was that the set of items would tap a broad array of reading skills and strategies.

Other teams included approximately fifteen individuals, typically instructors of English and literature, who critiqued and gave feedback on SAT items. One team got into the nuts and bolts of the statistical analyses that related item statistics with cognitive attributes, whereas another team explored methods in computational linguistics to generate or evaluate items. All of these consulting experiences gave me a profound appreciation of the methodologies and hard work required to create reading assessments.

This conclusion identifies ten future directions for improving reading assessments. It is an open question how practical it will be to implement these suggested directions, but it seems important to put them on the table for consideration.

1. Longer texts. Current reading assessments never get a snapshot of a reader lost in a book. Consider an absorbed reader on page 108 of a novel or a fascinating expository text. The reading experience involves cognitive and affective mechanisms that seem very different from an endless series of short isolated text segments (words, sentences, paragraphs, maybe three paragraphs) in most reading assessments. Short text segments involve an effortful construction of mental models (or situation models) from scratch; in contrast, an engaged reader of page 108 involves the reactivation, access, and integration of elements from a rich prior context, as well as an appreciation of the comprehension experience.

Reading assessments would benefit from an in-depth analysis of the reading of lengthy texts. What gets read? In what order? When do readers give up? What gets skipped? How much reading time is allocated to different text segments? What gets remembered? Computers can record all of such measures in fine detail.

2. Longer time spans of assessment. Reading assessments can be collected over months or years for individual readers. One obvious way to do this is to administer psychometrically validated reading tests at different points in time. This approach is advocated by nearly everyone, so the pressing questions are what tests to select, what infrastructure is needed to collect repeated assessments, and what time-dependent quantitative analyses are appropriate.

It is also possible to take a broader approach by collecting measures of courses, readings, quizzes, test scores, collaborations, projects, attendance, and other activities in an electronic, time-stamped portfolio for individual students. The measures provide assessments of motivation, learning rate, engagement, interest, self-regulated learning, world knowledge, and other constructs that typically are ignored. These measures can be correlated with scores on psychometric tests of reading.

3. A broader diversity of texts. Verbal comprehension items are skewed to the genres and interests of instructors of English literature, the primary population of item writers. Item writers are typically encouraged to include materials that cut across the academic curriculum (including science) and informal settings (e.g., newspapers, comics, legal documents), but progress on this has been modest. There needs to be an analysis of the corpus of documents that readers read or have access to. Text diversity is essential to assess the generality of particular reading skills and strategies.

4. Integration of text with multimedia. Most reading of younger generations is on electronic information sources with multimedia. A literate reader of today knows how to integrate the reading of text with these various forms of multimedia, as well as with other texts. Reading patterns can of course be recorded in fine detail with computer technologies.

5. Diverse assessment tasks. Alternative reading assessments will include a broad array of tasks and formats, including reading aloud, word naming, multiple choice, answers to open-ended questions, recall, summarization, statement verification, vocabulary recognition, cloze procedures, essays, the list goes on. It is important to conduct detailed cognitive task analyses that determine what cognitive components are affiliated with particular tasks/formats. Diverse tasks are needed to pinpoint general reading skills and strategies. Basic research is needed for advances in these areas.

6. Reading process measures. There is no reason to be confined to paper and pencil tests or human-recorded oral tests in this era of computer technologies. It possible to track reading processes at varying grain sizes through speech recognition, self-paced reading times, eye tracking, recording of keystrokes, verbal protocols (think aloud, self-explanations, question answering), evoked potentials, and computer tasks with embedded experimental manipulations. These process measures can be collected over time, with diverse tasks and materials, and correlated with psychometric tests of reading. Again, basic research is needed for advances in these areas.

7. Measures that tap deeper levels of comprehension. There are ample measures of language and decoding processes, vocabulary, interpretation of words in context, syntax, working memory, and basic cognitive processes. However, there needs to be more systematic measures at deeper levels of comprehension, such as semantic interpretation of clauses, inferences, cohesion, rhetorical structures, pragmatic impact of messages, and so on. Current items that tap deeper levels are based on the academic histories and intuitions of English instructors rather than theoretical frameworks in psycholinguistics, discourse processing, cognitive science, and other relevant scientific fields.

8. Measures that tap the full range of theoretical reading comprehension constructs. There are over a dozen reading constructs in contemporary scientific theories of reading. It is important to systematically construct and sample reading assessment items that tap the full range of constructs, following practices of evidence-centered design, for example. Ideally, subsets of items would differentiate each particular reading component and there would be an orthogonal variation of these constructs.

   However, it is widely acknowledged that these quantitative virtues are difficult to achieve because the constructs are highly correlated. Unfortunately, the history of psychometric practice has drifted to a small number of constructs (one to three, rather than fifteen) that are uniquely identifiable rather than doing justice to reading theories with complexity. New samples of items are often validated by comparing them with old banks of items that cover a narrow band of reading components (an unfortunate practice of item and construct inbreeding).

9. Psychometric methods that tap measures and parameters from data mining. Contemporary data-mining techniques collect information from large databases of performance measures, text corpora, sensory data, physiological recordings, environmental characteristics, and cognitive measures at a fine-grained level over time. These large databases are mined for quantitative parameters and qualitative states through data reduction and induction algorithms. The key question is how to translate these measures and parameters to trustworthy psychometric constructs.

10. Formative assessment and detailed reader profiles. Many have envisioned a world without summative tests of reading ability. Instead there would be formative assessment of reading components, diagnosis of deficits, and adaptive remediation of deficits through instruction and other learning experiences—all of this without the readers knowing they are being assessed in a high stakes test. These approaches already exist at a course grained level, but there is a question of how fine-grained the modeling can get with respect to particular theoretical constructs, individual differences, and classes of reading material. Answers to such questions require computer technologies and much more basic research.

Measuring Up:
Advances in How We Assess
Reading Ability: Editor Biographies

John Sabatini is a senior research scientist in the Center for Global Assessment, Research and Development Division at Educational Testing Service in Princeton, NJ. His research interests and expertise are in reading literacy development and disabilities, assessment, cognitive psychology, and educational technology, with a primary focus on adults and adolescents. Currently, he is the principal investigator of an Institute for Education Sciences funded grant to develop pre-K–12 comprehension assessments as part of the Reading for Understanding initiative. He is also principal investigator in an NICHD-funded Learning Disabilities Research Center project studying subtypes of reading disabilities in adolescents and recently completed a NICHD/Department of Education/National Institute for Literacy grant studying the relative effectiveness of reading programs for adults. He also serves as a coinvestigator on projects exploring the reading processes of adolescents, English language learners, and students with reading-based disabilities. He provides technical and research advice to national and international surveys including the National Assessments of Adult Literacy (NAAL), Programme for the International Assessment of Adult Competencies (PIAAC), and Progress in International Reading Literacy Study (PISA).

Dr. Sabatini was formerly an educational researcher at the National Center on Adult Literacy (NCAL) at the University of Pennsylvania. He received his doctorate at the University of Delaware in cognition and instruction with a focus on literacy and his bachelor's at the University of Chicago in behavioral science with a focus on neuropsychology.

Elizabeth Albro is currently the associate commissioner of the Teaching and Learning Division of the National Center for Education Research at the Institute of Education Sciences, U.S. Department of Education. Dr. Albro joined IES as an SRCD/AAAS Executive Branch Policy Fellow in 2002. Her responsibilities at IES have included serving as program officer for the Cognition and Student Learning, Reading and Writing Education, and Intervention for Struggling Adolescent and Adult Readers and Writers Research Programs. Throughout her research career, Dr. Albro has sought to build bridges across disciplines, and looked for ways to learn from both basic and applied research agendas. Exploring the development of children's ability to tell and understand stories as a window into comprehension processes was one line of research she pursued. In other research, she has used children's ability to narrate about goal-directed events to examine young children's memories of events with liked and disliked peers in early childhood, their understanding of the process of conflict resolution, and the role of teachers in fostering solutions to conflicts in the classrooms.

Prior to coming to the Institute, Dr. Albro was a member of the faculty in the Department of Psychology at Wheaton College in Norton, MA and in the Department of Education and Child Development at Whittier College in Whittier, CA. She received a B.A. in Behavioral Sciences, a M.A. in the Social Sciences and a Ph.D. in Psychology from the University of Chicago.

Tenaha O'Reilly is currently a research scientist in the Center for Global Assessment, Research and Development Division at Educational Testing Service. His research interests are broadly concerned with improving the validity of reading and writing assessments. In particular, he is interested in developing ways to measure and control for variables that may impact the interpretation of reading and writing scores. These variables include background knowledge, student interest and motivation, and print skill efficiency. Dr. O'Reilly is also interested in developing ways to use assessment as a tool for modeling students' learning, memory and transfer of ideas to novel situations. By blending the lessons learned from the domain of strategy instruction with assessment, assessments can be designed to both measure and support effective learning. To this aim, he has been a principal investigator and co-investigator on a number of projects geared towards developing cognitively based assessments of reading comprehension.

Dr. O'Reilly was formerly a researcher at the Institute for Intelligent Systems Literacy (IIS) at the University of Memphis. He received his doctorate at the University of Alberta in cognitive science with a focus on the application of prior knowledge and his bachelor's at Acadia University in psychology with a focus on reading strategy interventions.

Made in the USA
Middletown, DE
28 February 2019